STAGING YOUTH THEATRE

Rex Doyle

The Crowood Press

First published in 2003 by
The Crowood Press Ltd
Ramsbury, Marlborough
Wiltshire SN8 2HR

www.crowood.com

COLEG SIR GAR	
Cypher	16.02.04
792.0835	£14.99

British Library Cataloguing-in-Publication Data
A catalogue record for this book is available from the British Library.

ISBN 1 86126 604 9

Dedication
This book is dedicated to my family of vast proportions, but especially to Sandra, Candida,
Magnus, Daniel, Wanda and Mia.

Acknowledgements
Meg Jepson and the Sheffield Youth Theatre, without whom this book would not have been
possible and Tina Bicât for recommending me to The Crowood Press.
   Michael Alfreds, Gregory Thompson, Brian Way, David Glass, Peta Lily, Ayse Tashkaran,
Noam Meiri and Claudia Minne for their inspiration and countless exercises and strategies.
   Designers Colin Peters, Barry Jarvis and Rodney Ford for their help and practical
contributions, and Alan Boyle, Mark Dean, Sandra Voe, The Crucible Youth Theatre and
Sheffield Youth Theatre for their photographs.
   The staff and students, past and present, at The Guildford School of Acting.
   Peter James, Anthony Waller, Celia Greenwood and The Weekend Arts College,
The National Youth Theatre, The Chicken Shed, and Alan Rickman for contributing the
Foreword.

Typeset by Textype Typesetters, Cambridge

Printed and bound in Great Britain by Biddles Ltd, Guildford

CONTENTS

FOREWORD

I first met and worked with Rex Doyle at the Crucible Theatre, Sheffield, when he directed me in his own play about the life of the great dancer Nijinsky.

Everything that makes Rex such a fine director and teacher was evident in that production. Meticulous research and great leaps of imagination. But perhaps most importantly it was a production that was guided at all times by Rex's openness and generosity towards the actors and his boundless gift for encouragement. And it was fun. The rehearsal room was by definition a market place for common sense, fleeting instincts and mad ideas.

This excellent book is fed by exactly the same balance of the creative and the practical. Whether you need information on fund-raising, auditioning, running a rehearsal or making a prop, it is all here.

Youth Theatre continues to prove its worth not only in training young actors, directors and technicians, but also in developing the confidence and self-esteem of young people in a much wider sense. Dedicated youth leaders will benefit hugely from the guidance and inspiration which this book offers in abundance.

Alan Rickman

INTRODUCTION

This book is for anyone either already involved in or wishing to start a youth theatre. It is intended as a guide for the person who would like to direct a very simple nativity play or someone wanting to, or being asked to, venture upon the production of a classic or favourite musical.

There are chapters about technique, but only in the most simplistic terms, with suggestions for various exercises that can help to awaken the imagination and develop a strong sense of 'play' and self-discipline. Others give an awareness of space and time, of physical co-ordination and energy and of how the body works, of communicating both vocally and physically with clarity and feeling. Do not forget that youth orchestras and dance companies can achieve very high technical standards, and the same can be said about many Youth Theatres, but you must never let the student feel that they will be unable to achieve what you and they expect of themselves.

It is important when working with young people to have some knowledge of the craft of acting and directing but you are not training a young professional, and the function of a youth theatre for a lot of people is a step into adulthood. It is a wonderful way to forge new and lasting friendships, to gain confidence in oneself, to communicate with ease, and to discover one's voice.

Youth theatre also attracts students who have no desire to perform but still want to be part of that very special experience, and I will explain how they can make a big contribution to the whole event. The building and painting of scenery, the designing and making of costumes and props, the publicity and marketing, are all jobs that need to be carried out before you can launch a successful production and there is no reason why members of the youth theatre cannot be involved here as well.

For the director there are hints on suitable material, on how to make the best use of available space and transform your school hall or scout hut into a theatre. Of what to do with vast numbers of eager students who want to be 'in' the play, but for one reason or another cannot cope with the responsibility of a speaking part. There are practical approaches to the preparation of texts for rehearsals, and the creation of a production team.

You may wonder at what age it is best for a young person to join a youth theatre. This is a difficult question to answer, as a company with a wide age range often produces a very healthy ensemble. Younger students have daring and vivid imaginations that are unhampered by the onset of puberty, whereas teenagers are longing to separate themselves from childhood but are unable to face the full responsibility of adulthood.

If you are operating from within a school, where timetabling and availability make it easier for you to draw your company from a particular year, Chapter 1 will help you with setting up your company, and Chapter 2 will give you ideas for exercises. The older the student/actor the more he or she becomes aware of technique. Details of how to look for funding and on the complex process of auditions is also covered in Chapter 1. Working with younger students can be very rewarding, and their ability to improvise can produce some very creative results, but they find the process of rehearsal tedious. There are suggestions on how to retain their interest, whilst working towards an end product, and on the use of movement and mime as a method of storytelling.

There comes a time, however, when a member will grow out of youth theatre. A chosen career in banking or medicine, working in a supermarket, becoming a hairdresser, a mother, or an air stewardess will be more important to a young person than becoming an actress or a lighting designer. Only those who find a true inner vocational fire will want to pursue their knowledge of acting further, and they of course will be motivated to further their studies by training at a drama school, studying for a drama degree at university or getting into one of the National Youth Theatre's productions.

One must not forget that music can enhance a production, and that the writing, playing and recording of it is another area of involvement. If you choose to mount a musical do not forget the importance of a musical director, with live musicians to interpret and play the all-important score.

There is something special about a youth theatre event that is very difficult to describe until you have experienced it, either from being within the performance or from participating as a member of the audience. The most satisfying results are arrived at when a sense of discipline, respect, humility and love is shared in bringing the chosen material to life.

1   CREATING A COMPANY

Whether you are starting from scratch or putting your youth theatre on a more permanent footing, this chapter offers you choices and practical advice, from the recruitment of cast and crew to fund-raising and the timing of the rehearsal period. Some suggestions may appear to be quite formal, but it is well to remember that the theatre, even in these enlightened days, is often viewed with suspicion and disapproval. Everything possible should be done to ensure that the participants have a safe, fair and enlightened journey, and that their parents and guardians know they are being more than adequately cared for.

CREATING A YOUTH THEATRE IN A SCHOOL OR COLLEGE

Let us assume that you are working in a school with an age range of eleven to eighteen years, catering for both boys and girls. You have been approached or would like to produce a play using the pupils from the school. Previous productions have been infrequent and have met with varying degrees of success. The School Play was always directed by the geography master who has now left.

Before making any announcement, find out who will be sympathetic to your plans, and try to avoid false rumours filtering through to the pupils. As soon as you have a concrete plan, approach the Principal and find out if he or she approves. In a well-equipped school there are a number of very useful resources on hand – for example, the art department for help with design, the music department, home economics for the making of costumes, the wood- and metalwork department for scenery. Help from any of these departments could be invaluable, but make it clear to those who are interested that the project is for, and by, the young actors, and not for their own glorification. Also make good friends with the caretaker, because his co-operation will be invaluable when you are getting into the final stages of rehearsal.

Don't Do Too Much

Whatever your role in the school, the play and all its jobs can soon become overwhelming. It is important that you do not let your new role as youth theatre director interfere with your usual commitments and responsibilities. Try to organize your work ahead of time – preparing your lessons and releasing yourself from additional tasks. Make sure you have allies on whom you can call for help when the pressure of production becomes too much.

THE EARLY DAYS

Your first priority should be to create a list of possible plays that the company could perform. You may have chosen one already or the Principal might have asked you to direct something of his choice. If you need more ideas there are some suggestions in Chapter 3, and Chapter 5 will help you make a decision about where and how you will eventually present your production. What you should be looking for is an ensemble of eager, committed young actors who will feel at home in the choice of play – one that is not over-ambitious and that they would be happy to do.

Once you have had the go-ahead from those in authority you will need to look very carefully at the school calendar, taking note of examination dates, holidays and other official school events. Make sure that your production is put on the calendar and that you have booked the venue in which the production is to take place, giving yourself adequate time for technical and dress rehearsal.

If there is a drama studio book it for one or two evenings a week, and then advertise a series of drama sessions or workshops that are available for all those interested throughout the school, making it very clear what will happen at these sessions and how long they will last. These workshops could be oversubscribed so keep the numbers down to a workable group. It is more fruitful to have more sessions with less people than trying to work with too many at one time. In Chapter 2 a number of exercises are described in detail that will help you to structure these preliminary workshops. These exercises will also give some idea of the talent that is available and the willingness of the potential actor to absorb and take direction. Be patient with those who are eager but not very talented. They could contribute a great deal to the venture.

Some people will attend out of curiosity, others will be very eager to participate but may not be free for rehearsals and all the scheduled performances. Prepare some audition/workshop forms before you start work, and make sure everyone has one and that you have collected the completed forms before the end of the session. Some people will want to be involved on the technical side, and though you may not need them for all the creative workshops their encouragement, involvement and availability are essential to the success of the production.

SCHEDULING THE REHEARSALS PERIOD

The following timetabling will give you some idea of how to organize the time spent on rehearsal. Let us assume that the production is scheduled for a week during the Michaelmas term, preferably immediately after the mid-term break.

Audition Workshops

Find a time during the summer term to hold the audition workshops. They should start half an hour after school finishes and last for an hour and a half. Both you and the students will be tired after a hard day's work, so try to pick a

Short Rehearsal Periods

With a youth theatre the best results can happen with a shorter, intensive rehearsal period, rather than long tiring hours of waiting around that test the endurance of both director and actor. Important things will not be forgotten especially if your preliminary workshops have been carefully planned.

A CHRISTMAS CAROLE

WORKSHOP/AUDTIONS

These will be held in **THE DRAMA STUDIO** the weeks beginning **8th JULY** and the **15th JULY.**
Those students interested in being part of the **TECHNICAL STAFF** attend on **MONDAY 8th or 15th JULY @ 4.30 p.m.**
Those students interested in **PERFORMING** please attend on **WEDNESDAY 10th or 17th JULY, or THURSDAY 11th or 18th JULY @ 4.30 p.m.**

TO PERFORMERS.
Please come suitably dressed, and bring with you a paragraph from A CHRISTMAS CAROLE by CHARLES DICKENS that you have read and are familiar with but not learnt, and any instrument you can play.

ALL YEAR GROUPS WELCOME

Please sign below.

TECHNICAL STAFF (Wardrobe, Props, Scenery, Lighting, Sound and Stage Management)

MONDAY 8th JULY	MONDAY 15th JULY
PERFORMERS.	
WEDNESDAY 10th JULY	WEDNESDAY 17th JULY
THURSDAY 11th JULY	THURSDAY 18th JULY

4.30 p.m. @ THE DRAMA STUDIO

Sample notice for workshops.

NATIONAL YOUTH THEATRE OF GREAT BRITAIN-AUDITION FORM 2002

PLEASE FILL IN THE SECTIONS MARKED ➡IN BLOCK CAPITALS USING BLACK OR BLUE INK.

➡SECTION ONE: PERSONAL DETAILS......

➡Surname:	➡First Name (s):
➡Permanent Address:	➡Present Address (e.g. term time):
➡Tel No(s):	➡Tel No(s):
➡Date of Birth:	➡Age:
➡ Email Address:	

SECTION TWO: THE AUDITION.....

➡Department (please tick one)			➡Date:		
➡Acting ☐	➡Stage Management ☐	➡Costume ☐	➡Lighting and Sound ☐	➡Workshop ☐	➡Administration ☐
Location:			Interviewer:		
Acting Piece 1➡_____			Acting Piece 2➡_____		

SECTION THREE	

SECTION FOUR: ROUND TWO.....

LOCATION:	DATE:	INTERVIEWER:
ASSESSMENT:		
RESULT:		

PLEASE TURN OVER

....

.... ↘

Audition form from National Youth Theatre.

SECTION FIVE......➡

➡Name and Address of School/College:			
➡Type of Institution(please circle)	STATE SCHOOL	INDEPENDENT SCHOOL	COLLEGE/UNIVERSITY

➡If you are A Level/GCSE/IB Student, which Shakespeare Texts are you currently studying?

➡Present Employment (if applicable):

➡Future Plans (e.g. University, training, employment , travel)

➡Hobbies, Special Skills and Capabilities (e.g. Sports, Languages etc)

➡Theatre Experience (including school productions, musicals etc)

➡Musical Instruments played, including any grades achieved

➡Can you sing? If yes please state your range (if known)

➡Can you dance? If yes state details of any training/qualifications received.

➡How did you hear about National Youth Theatre? Please tick one of the following......

➡Teacher ☐	➡Poster ☐	➡Friend ☐	➡Website ☐	➡Newspaper ☐	➡Radio/TV ☐
➡Other (please specify)...					

➡Did you use the National Youth Theatre recorded information line? (please tick).........
YES ☐ NO ☐
If yes did you find it useful?_____

➡In order to implement our equal opportunities policy, we would be grateful if you would tick one of the following boxes, that best describes your ethnic origin. (please note that this information will be treated in the strictest confidence and is for office use only)

➡White ☐	➡Mixed ☐	➡Asian or Asian British ☐	➡Black or Black British ☐	➡Chinese or other ☐

13

day or days early in the week. However, the timing of these sessions may prove difficult with examinations going on. Pick a time when the age group you would like to work with are under less pressure. After the workshops are over let the successful actors know in writing that you are offering them a place in the company, and make sure that they formally accept it. Also inform the reserve actors in case people drop out between the auditions and the rehearsals. Rather than choose understudies it can be appropriate to double cast the production. You will find more about this later in the book. Use this period also to start selecting your technical team.

First Rehearsal Period

A three-week rehearsal period should take place towards the end of the summer break, Sunday to Friday with Saturdays off, a total of eighteen days. Or alternatively two weeks, Sunday to Sunday with no break which will give you fifteen days. Try to keep the length of the days as close to school hours as possible, as this is how the students are programmed to work. If they get tired the concentration goes and the actors become unfocused and restless. The morning session could be 9.00–12.00 with one hour for lunch. (Actors should bring a packed lunch and plenty of water. Organize the mealtime formally and encourage conversation and mixing.) The afternoon session should last from 1.00–3.30 or 4.00. There could be some learning, research or study to be accomplished after rehearsals and remember both you and the actors will get tired, but not weary or bored if the work is well planned with plenty of action and variety of activity.

Second Rehearsal Period

Rehearsals will need to continue during the beginning of the Michaelmas term, but only on one or two evenings a week, with a whole day on Sundays. By this time the play will be taking shape and you will be in a position to start running whole sections. Do this on the Sunday and leave the weekday sessions for those scenes with only a few actors in them as they will most likely need individual attention.

Final Rehearsals into Production

Half-term is another intensive period for one week, Sunday to Sunday, or less if you feel things are in good shape. You could work full days as before with the technical staff now integrated into building the set, preparing the props and organizing the costumes and dress rehearsals. The first week after half-term will be for final dress rehearsals and performances. If you need to take students out of classes make sure you have checked with the involved members of staff. If you want an audience for a dress rehearsal during school hours make sure it is possible and that it has been authorized by the Principal.

Hopefully the production should be well subscribed as you have a captive audience, and a big cast automatically brings in family and friends. Make sure you have organized front-of-house personnel and there are interval refreshments.

OTHER POSSIBILITIES

A teacher working with students either in specified drama classes, or using drama as a tool to teach English, studying plays, poetry and creative writing may want to present a short piece of work. It is possible to give them the opportunity of presenting their work to the rest of the school but in a less formal manner, and this could quite easily be presented in the drama studio with a limited audience. It would not require sophisticated lighting, and could be costumed in a very simply manner. It would give the younger actors a chance to show their mettle as

Sheffield Youth Theatre.

performers. Conversely, senior students, with gaps between taking examinations, could perform dramatized excerpts from books and plays being studied lower down the school, or take a short original play or adapted folk tale into the feeder schools.

The Independent Youth Theatre

To start an independent Youth Theatre requires dedication on the part of the director and a great deal of planning. You will need support not only morally but financially and practically, so it is a good idea to find one or two like-minded people who will support your ideas, and put in the much-needed work, for at this stage your rewards will not be financial ones. The following suggestions may be of use to you.

Youth Clubs

Offer your services to your local Youth Club. Suggest if they haven't done any drama that you do a one-off session. You will get ideas in Chapter 2, or you may have your own ideas. This will test the ground for enthusiasm and commitment and will also give you an opportunity to find out how the club members respond to you and your ideas.

Local Libraries

A visit to the local libraries will give you access to a lot of information. They will have information about youth theatres and clubs in your district. There will also be information about other classes that are being held locally. A voice teacher or an expert in yoga or one of the physical disciplines may be interested in

15

Library notice board.

helping in your venture. A friendly visit or joining the class will give you an idea of the kind of spaces available for hire that you could use for rehearsal or performance, and the qualities of the teacher.

Local Schools

Locate the drama-friendly schools and make contact with teachers who are interested or already teaching drama. Try and see some school productions. This will give you an idea of the standard of youth theatre in your district, and the kind of venues available for performance. The more you can co-operate with schools the better. A supportive and sympathetic school will help you in recruiting

members for your youth theatre, and they may also be willing to advertise auditions and so forth.

Youth Theatre Committee

Organize a small committee of like-minded people, comprising a good cross-section of the community, including teachers, parents, even the local vicar and, of course, potential members. A friendly solicitor would be an invaluable member. This committee will not be concerned with the artistic policy, but will take responsibility for the financial and practical aspects of the organization. Minutes need to be kept, and a treasurer appointed. A simple mission statement could be drawn up that will help to keep the organization focused on its aims and objectives, and is useful when approaching commercial and professional organizations.

Public Funding and Support

Enquire at your local education and council offices about any possible financial support, and friendly venues that have been equipped to accommodate touring theatre productions. Find out if they would be interested in supporting your venture, by giving your production house room, and the cost of hiring the space.

Your Local Theatre

Arrange to meet the Artistic Director of your local theatre and find out if he is interested in co-operating with you. It is important to know whether the theatre produces and mounts its own productions, or merely receives touring productions. There may be a youth theatre attached to the organization, so try to meet the director or person in charge. Be careful what you say if you have seen some of their work and have not liked it. You are in the land of egos and competition and you do not need to make enemies. Also be careful what you say about your own plans and ideas. If the director is well established and has financial support, you might find that your ideas are stolen before you have the time and money to realize them. It is not only what you do but the care and consideration that you give to your company, and the journey you can take them on.

The Media

Get to know your local journalists and radio presenters. A slot on local radio is a good way of advertising what you are going to do and it is for free. Tact and diplomacy is paramount when dealing with the media. Remember, for them you are only a news item, and a clever interviewer can lead you into saying things that could be taken the wrong way.

FINANCING THE PRODUCTION

There is no question that you are going to need money. Not a lot, but you will need it for the hire of halls, for postage, for publicity, for royalties, for building materials, costumes and props and scripts. Let us take a look at the various ways in which you can raise money. Your committee can be of enormous help but first of all find out what you can get for free, and make a list.

Sponsorship

During your research period you may have found some money made available through the council and education departments. Public money is hard to win and you need to be careful that you show how you have invested it. There may be some local charities that donate sums of money to youth organizations. This may require you to write a letter of application and your committee will help you with this. A local firm might be interested in sponsoring your production. This could allow you to be more ambitious, but remember there may be strings attached that could limit your scope and artistic choices. You will have to acknowledge all sponsors by displaying their logo on all your material. You will need to find out what it is they require before sending out any official publicity.

Fund-Raising

This can be done in the conventional ways with raffles, sponsored sporting events, T-shirts and so on. Publicized events can help, but however brilliant they may be, make sure they are cost-effective. You could start a 'Friend of the Youth Theatre' committee that could help with fund-raising events, and it is a way of involving parents and interested parties, but do not let these subsidiary committees dictate what the company should be doing.

Subscription and Audition Fees

Depending on the company's financial position you might find it necessary to gather some income from auditions and for the actual production. If you are anticipating a huge response you will need to formalize the recruitment and audition process and this would entail some income to cover administrative costs such as postage, phone calls and so on. To give an example, the NYT charge a £10 audition fee, and the successful applicants then have to attend a three-week acting course before they can be considered for casting in a production.

Box Office

An estimate of how much you can expect from the sale of tickets will have to be included in your budgets. This means knowing where you are going to perform and the number of seats you are hoping to sell. During your early research find out how much people are prepared to pay. It will be one of the company's tasks to sell tickets to friends, relatives and

A theatre box office (the Crucible).

members of the public. You have to be strict as everyone loves performing but no one enjoys selling tickets, however, you will need every penny you can get.

SCHEDULING THE PRODUCTION

Great care must be taken in the timing of your production. Your company will be drawn not only from many different schools, but individuals who have taken their official holiday to work with the youth theatre. It is therefore advisable to plan your production for the summer holidays. You will only have about three weeks for rehearsal and not more than two, or at the most three, weeks for performances. All-day, everyday sessions will be necessary to get through the work, but watch the energy levels of the company. Push them when they are lazy, but not when they are exhausted. Give them time to relax and eat, and make sure they are getting enough sleep.

The days should be divided into sessions. If you are going to work them into the evening, organize two breaks. They should bring a packed meal for one of them, as large numbers of people going out and getting sandwiches

can waste time. They should have something more substantial in the second break as they will get very hungry and begin to lose concentration and energy. Rehearsal discipline will be covered in later chapters, but the following suggestion will give you some idea how to organize your time: 9.30–12.30 (short break for a drink); 12.30–1.30 (packed lunch and fresh air); 1.30–4.30 (short break for drink); 4.30–6.00 (hot meal and fresh air) 6.00–8.00 (no break), then home.

I suggest for this type of production you have an age limit of 13–21. Some of those who are younger can easily cope but you have to remember the concerns of parents when young people are travelling home on their own late in the evening.

THE AUDITION PROCESS

There are many ways of auditioning a company. The method suggested in the preceding example can work with an ad hoc company, but I will outline some formal approaches that will give you an opportunity to select what is important for you.

Where It Is to Be Held

Make sure you have booked a hall well in advance, and that people know where it is and the time you expect them to be there. They should come prepared with their audition pieces learnt and with suitable clothing and footwear, something that is easy to move in but doesn't hide the body.

An Ensemble Company

If you are looking for an ensemble to perform a play like *Doomsday* from the *Mysteries* by Tony Harrison you might give everyone the same piece of the text to prepare for the audition. You would then call groups of people and work with them for a selected period of time to find out how they respond to being part of a group.

A Shakespeare Classic or More Traditional Play

If the play is by Shakespeare you might select a speech for the girls to learn and one for the boys, or a passage of dialogue and call them in pairs, and see how they work together.

The Straight Audition with Interview

You could ask them to prepare two pieces – one modern and one from the classical repertoire – and audition them separately. This would allow you to talk to the prospective company member and put them at their ease. It would allow you to mix those interested in the technical side with the actors, and clarify their availability for the rehearsal and performance dates.

The Audition Form

Prepare an audition form similar to the one I suggested earlier in the chapter, that will include all the necessary information, and spaces for the prospective company member to put in their details. This will have to be completed before you can proceed with an offer. So make sure you have contact numbers and the approval of a responsible adult (ideally a parent or guardian). Those people selected to join the company will have to make some financial contribution to the venture, and how that money is to be paid must be made clear in the form. The whole process of selection is stressful for both parties so keep calm, be punctual and well organized. If not, you could either end up seeing no one at all or be swamped with gatecrashers.

THE RECALL AND ACCEPTANCE LETTER

After the general auditions you might want to have a recall system or have already built one into your audition process. You can tell people that you want to recall them at the first audition, but make sure they do not mistake it for an offer to join the company. Offering a place in the company should be done with a letter after the auditions. Wait for the acceptance or refusal before you offer their place to someone else. It is important for everyone to know where they stand, as a rejection is hard to accept especially when you are young.

THE 'ONE-OFF' EVENT

Boy Scouts, Guides, Sunday schools, amongst many youth organizations, are often approached to perform events at certain times of the year. This event is something more

---

Quality Work

Competition and ambition are driving forces producing exciting work, but they should not be the only qualities a youth theatre should have; sincerity, truthfulness, dedication and an ability to communicate with others are equally important factors.

Dear ....

Thank you for auditioning for us. I am very pleased to inform you that you have been successful and we would like to offer you a place in our company:
(a) To play as cast.
(b) To perform the role of .... and play as cast.
(c) To join the technical team.

REHEARSALS will start on Monday 29 July @ 10.00 for three weeks (Sundays included).
PERFORMANCES are at the Civic Theatre from Tuesday 19 August to Saturday 24 August @ 7.30 with a matinée on Saturday 24 August @ 2.30.

Signature of the attached acceptance form confirms that you are available for all these dates, and that we receive the necessary fees stated on the booking form before or on the first days of rehearsals. (Cheques should be made payable to the Castlebridge Youth Theatre.) Failure to return the signed form within a week of receiving this letter will of course mean that your place in the company will no longer be kept open.
If you do not wish to join the company please complete the non-acceptance box and return the form to us, as other people are waiting to join the company.

I accept the offer of a place in the CASTLEBRIDGE YOUTH THEATRE COMPANY and am available from MONDAY 29 July until SATURDAY 24 August.

Signed ....

I do not accept a place in the CASTLEBRIDGE YOUTH THEATRE COMPANY.

Signed ....

A sample acceptance letter.

THE RESERVE LIST LETTER.

Dear ....

Thank you for auditioning for us. We enjoyed your work, but are unable to offer you a place at the moment. However, we are putting you on our reserve list, and if anyone is unable to attend the rehearsals and performances we would consider offering you a place. Please return the attached form to let us know whether you are still interested and available for all the dates.

I am available from Monday 29 July until Saturday 24 August and would like to be put on the reserve list.

Signed ....

THE REFUSAL LETTER.

Dear.........................

Thank you for auditioning for the company. I am sorry that we are unable to offer you a place in our Company this year. However, please continue to audition for future productions and if you are interested in our other projects we can put you on our mailing list.

Reserve list and refusal letters.

formal than a presentation at a school assembly, and is often only a short piece of drama or storytelling with music, songs and movement. If you find yourself responsible for organizing such an event I would encourage you to give it your fullest attention. If well presented and planned it allows the young actor to perform with clarity and sincerity, and also with their own voice.

The Company

Ideally everyone should be involved in the presentation, but make sure that you keep one or two evenings free for preparation and rehearsal. Don't let this become a burden. The older members can help the younger ones. Find time for them to explore the material in small groups. Choose suitable songs, put new lyrics to familiar tunes or vice versa and create dances. With younger members the story can be developed through movement and mime. Create large rod puppets that can move to a spoken text or carol. This will work well in churches and halls with poor sight-lines (*see* chapters four and five for practical help). Think pageant rather than play.

The Venue for Rehearsals

If your club has a permanent base you are at an advantage, because you will not have to look for rehearsal space. However, you will need to have a peaceful atmosphere in which to prepare your presentation, so make sure that everyone is involved when you plan to rehearse, rather than try to work against people playing snooker or table tennis in the same space. A great deal of enjoyment can be derived from making costumes and props, but remember to try the ideas out at home beforehand rather than experiment in the moment.

The Venue for Performance

Study the venue carefully. Make drawings and plans and also take measurements if necessary.

Have a clear idea of how you are going to stage the event, and allow one or, if possible, two sessions in the performance venue with the company so that they can see how the event is going to work with an audience. Try to avoid having a sophisticated lighting plot and having too many props or costume changes. Supply everyone with a written notice of the place and times of the performances. Make sure that there is also a clear map and directions of how to get to the venue, and that the younger members will be collected at the end of the performance and are not left to find their way home, by themselves.

Whatever your production is going to be, from some poetry performed at a memorial service to a performance of *The Tempest* in the grounds of a stately home, you should now be ready to plan rehearsals.

Sheffield Youth Theatre *performing* **Romeo and Juliet.**

21

2 WORKING TOGETHER

The previous chapter gave you some idea about how to organize your time into workable sessions. This chapter is about filling those sessions with activities that are not only enjoyable and absorbing, but also revealing. It will cover games and exercises that you will be able to use when starting with your company or during the workshops you may hold when you are auditioning. It is important to know what effect these exercises and games are having on the actors and where they are leading them. You will discover qualities in the participants that would never be apparent in a more conventional one-to-one encounter. The natural leaders begin to emerge, the generous person, the silent listener, the enthusiast and the 13-year-old covered in embarrassment, the shy and the extrovert. There is also a place for those with special difficulties. The exercises described in this chapter are primarily for creatively opening up the mind, body and imagination, whereas those in Chapter 6 are about preparation for rehearsal and performance. You also need to know what you are looking for in terms of talent in the individual and the potential of the group. Some people find this work difficult, and resent the pressure of participation without having a role to hide behind. They could be highly talented, but not suitable material for an ensemble.

First Aid

It is important to have a trained 'Firstaider' as part of your team in the event of an accident or a member being taken ill, and a well-equipped First-Aid Box. This should contain rubber gloves, scissors, lint, bandages for dressings and sprains, squares of material for slings, sterile burn dressings, arnica ointment for bruises and sprains, a packet of plasters. Though pain-killers like paracetamol will be requested for headaches they should not be administered by you. Check with parents and guardians about members of the company with chronic illness like epilepsy, asthma, diabetes and allergies and who are on special medication.

THE FIRST MEETING

Starting the first session can cause problems as you might be shy and nervous. The people arriving are also unsure of what is happening. Some may have come along with a friend, whilst others may be with an anxious parent who is concerned about what their child is getting involved in. A few young actors you already know, or who appeared in a previous production, can assist in breaking down shyness and making those early moments easier. Rather than taking a register, suggest to

Students wearing labels doing a mirror exercise (Sheffield Youth Theatre).

them that they fill in the forms I mentioned in the previous chapter, so have plenty of pens available. This will help if there are any changes of address or phone number. It is also a good way of breaking the ice.

Sticky Labels

On the first day everyone should have a label stuck to their T-shirt with their name clearly written on so that everyone can read it. These labels should always be worn until a date decided upon by the group when they can be removed.

Encourage people to help each other in filling in the form. Let them know where the lavatories are, and the boys' and girls' changing rooms.

The helpers can remind individuals about security, about leaving money and valuables (like watches and mobile phones) in vulnerable places, which could create a temptation to the light-handed.

Greeting the Company

When everybody has changed into working clothes, assemble the company. There will

Dress Code

Insist that people are suitably dressed at all times. No tight jeans, soft footwear or bare feet, with hair tied back and out of the eyes, and no jewellery, especially earrings that can get caught in clothing or hair and cause damaged ear lobes. Make sure that the clothing is washable and that the wearer is not concerned about damage or wear and tear and that the girls wear either trousers or tights under skirts. An ankle-length full practice skirt is a useful article of clothing. They should also bring plenty of still water to drink.

always be a few late-comers, so let one of your helpers look after them. If you have a chair for everyone suggest they sit down. Most of the sessions will be executed on the floor with nothing to sit on, but a chair to start with offers security, and is treating everyone as equals, and in an adult way. A simple greeting is all that is needed, and a brief description of

The listening circle

what the day, or days will involve, which leads very simply into the first exercise. Getting rid of the chairs and any personal belongings should be done with the minimum of speech.

The First Exercise

Listening is very important and an excellent starting place for any session. It helps to focus the actors' attention and clear the mind of disturbance. Begin with everyone standing in a circle with their eyes closed. Observe how people join in, from the first eager participant to the last few stragglers. Once the circle is formed and the eyes are closed listen to the sounds within the room, and then slowly enlarge the circle of listening to outside the room until it is focused on the farthest sound you can hear, and beyond. Allow the listening to last for a few moments and then bring it back to the beating of the heart and the natural rhythm of breathing. The eyes are then opened and comments are invited as to what was experienced.

Sharing the Experience

It is good practice to have a post-mortem after completing an exercise. The ability to articulate and report what is felt and seen is essential for them to develop a sense of judgement and to make observations without being negative. It could have gone really well and the actor needs to see that it has. Things may not have gone as was expected, so this needs to be expressed as well. Encourage them to make observations rather than criticisms and to take advantage of the spontaneous action, and make it work. Phrases such as 'That was crap', or 'It was rubbish', should be avoided at all times.

Sharing the experience – Ase Tashkarin with some students at the Guildford School of Acting.

Name Learning

As director, it is essential for you to learn everyone's name as soon as possible. Make sure you have a register with you, as it helps with the task of remembering the order of events and particulars of individual behaviour. These facts can easily be forgotten in the excitement of a drama session, and you are there to discover as much as you can about each individual. It is also important for the group to get to know each other's names.

Unless you encourage it to happen, people will stick together with their preferred group of 'friends' rather than mixing with everybody. The name on the T-shirt may not always tally with the name on the form or register, so getting to know the name everyone wants to be known by is the next task.

Going Round the Circle

Build the names as you go round. Person A will start by introducing himself to the group and to his next-door neighbour B. He then finds out B's name. B repeats his name and introduces A to C. C repeats A and B's names, her own name, and then introduces D, and so on round the circle. With a large group this can take some time. People can be mean and withhold their name by putting their hand over their label, or they can be generous and leave the circle to move nearer and help someone having trouble in remembering a difficult name.

Handy Workshop Tools

Useful props to have at one's disposal during workshops and rehearsals include: one-medium-sized basketball; a cassette or CD player; 18 plain wood broom handles; 18 tennis balls; lots of scrap paper; lots of pens and pencils.

If the group is being reticent, it is up to you to make something of every exercise, and to see the drama in very simple activities, so encouraging a sense of play is important. It is not just the learning of the name that is interesting; it is everyone's attitude to saying and hearing their own name spoken.

Saying the Names and Throwing the Ball

We can now add movement to the learning of the names. It is also time to get everyone up and moving. Invite the company to stand. Take the basketball, throw it up in the air and observe it bouncing. Keep the focus on the ball until it comes to rest. This can take a while. Ask when the ball ceases to live. Ask who gives it life. Suggest that the ball symbolizes the text, and that we, the actors, give it life. The ball is then thrown from one actor to another using the names of the participants as the text. Let us imagine that three of the actors are called

---

Remembering Everyone's Name

This is essential when working with large groups of people. Being addressed by your name has a magical effect upon the ego; conversely, always being called by the wrong name or just 'you' is nearly always taken as an insult or a rejection.

Saying names and throwing the ball.

Robert, Sarah and Tracey. The following dialogue should be used:

ROBERT (holding the ball, and still in the circle): Robert to . . . (He contacts Sarah with a look. He throws the ball to her saying her name) . . . Sarah.
This should be done accurately and with care. The ball must not be dropped. Sarah will then contact another member of the group, say TRACEY with a look.
SARAH (now in possession of the ball says) Sarah to Tracey . . . The ball is thrown to Tracey and so the game continues.

If it is going smoothly let them play for a while until everyone has been involved. Note the names and people who keep being in possession of the ball. If people are not speaking clearly, not using eye contact before the name is said, or the ball is thrown badly, and they are playing tricks on each other, you should stop the game, and register your observation. Compliment them on their sense of fun and play but ask them to find that within the disciplines of the game. If for any reason some members of the group are unable to deal with the ball, suggest the group find a way of including everybody in the game.

To give the exercise more energy and excitement encourage them to move about the space. Reiterate that the set of rules made earlier are obeyed. There should be clear communication between thrower and receiver,

Inclusivity

Sheffield Youth Theatre students.

You may find that people with some impairment will want to be part of the youth theatre but will find it different to join. Everybody has something in their make-up that is not perfect, but this does not mean that they are unable to achieve perfection. Do not compromise the work, but let the group find a way of including everyone in what is happening. Someone may have to become somebody else's eyes, another, somebody's ears, legs or hands. One piece of work will suit one group of people, another piece another group. So before you find yourself saying no to someone, just consider what their presence in the group may bring to the quality of the work.

and the thrower's name should always be spoken clearly. The focus is always with the speaker and alters with the movement of the ball. This is essential once the game gains momentum.

Suggest they are now playing a spectator sport, and they are a first-class team. Encourage bravado and skill. Don't let a dropped ball destroy the atmosphere. You have now added an imaginary world and a suggestion of character. It is now time for another direction. Suggest that when you bang the drum the game goes into slow motion, both vocally and physically. You have now introduced the question of time, and its importance in the theatre. Once slow motion is established, alternate it with normal time.

If the game is still being dominated by a few 'Smart Alecs', take them out of the action, but give them the role of manager or promoter, which will allow the shy or reticent one a chance to participate more actively, and still give the brighter eager actor a role to play in the game.

So in one simple exercise we are not only learning each other's names but learning about focus, the use of energy and an awareness of space. Later in the workshop you can apply many variations to this exercise. It can be used to bring energy back into the group, especially when played with two teams, for example girls versus boys. If used with text from the play you are rehearsing or studying it helps to see where the text is going and how it is received. When played with energy but as the characters of the play, the difference between your own rhythm and that of the character becomes very clear.

TRUST

Being able to trust each other is essential in producing focused, exciting work. The following exercise is excellent for putting trust in someone else, developing an awareness of the senses and seeing one's environment from an entirely new perspective. Choose a partner. One becomes blind whilst the other partner is going to be responsible for taking care of them. There are many variations of this exercise. You can use the room you are working in, or the blind participant can be taken out of the building. The sighted one needs to be very sensitive to the needs of their partner. They will sense immediately how their blind partner is responding to the exercise.

Moving your Partner by Touch
The sighted person stands in front of the blind partner, and gently takes the hands palm to palm with his hands underneath. The sighted one now very gently moves the blind partner's hands and arms, drawing them forward or backward with very subtle changes of direction and pressure. Let the pairs discover

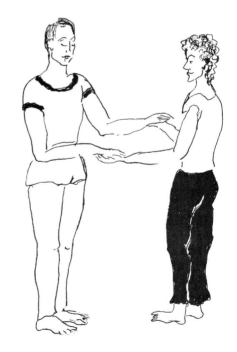

Moving your partner by touch

27

the extremities of the movements they can achieve. They will eventually be able to move freely round the room, to guide their partner to the floor to move them forwards and backwards.

Having achieved this, the sighted partner now moves the blind partner with a gentle push in a specific part of their body, the back of the shoulder, behind the knee, the side of the face, and the partner responds to this stimulus and finds where and when the movement comes to rest.

Exploring the Environment

This is another variation on the above exercise. It is a less intense exercise, still requiring trust, and shows that when denied one sense, the others compensate for it by becoming more intense. The participants need concentration and integrity, otherwise the exercise disintegrates into a silly game. The sighted person becomes the blind partner's guide. Give them a chance to explore the room. Let them feel the texture of, for example, the curtains and the metal door handle, and forewarn them about a step up or down. This exercise is best executed in a silent environment, so the sensitivity experienced in the first exercise can be applied here. You want the participants to become aware of their sense of touch, of sounds around them, the warmth and light of sun on their faces, and the change in the texture of the flooring.

Before you allow them to change partners, have the customary chat to share what has been discovered. Some will not have liked the experience, others will have really enjoyed it. If there is easy access to the outside and the weather is good, taking your blind partner outside can be interesting and exciting. You could go to a favourite place, a seat in a garden, down by the river, or even to the perfume counter in a big department store. Don't tell them where, and leave them for a moment just to focus on what they can hear and sense. On

Written Experiences

Sometimes it is valuable to record the actor's experiences before they are talked about. If you want to do this have your scraps of paper and pens at the ready. After the improvisation or stimulus is over, do not encourage conversation. Tell them to collect their paper and pen, find a place on the floor to write, then put pen to paper and let it flow. Do not allow them to question the activity, but just to write. Allow about ten minutes for the activity. If they finish sooner, ask them to put the pen down and wait. When time is up, get them to underline their favourite line or phrase. These are then spoken randomly but not together. As confidence grows, more and more text is spoken. Collect the papers once the exercise is over as you might want to use them in other exercises.

returning to base the closed eyes are opened and the experience recalled. The observations are very interesting. Partners change roles and the exercise is repeated.

There are many other exercises involving trust. The company works in groups of three. The two outside people stand facing the third person who is in the middle with their eyes closed. The two on the outside begin to gently push the middle person backwards and forwards, making sure they feel secure and can take the middle person's weight easily. They are not to drop the middle person, but to give them a smooth experience. Of course, the one being moved has to keep their knees locked and their spine held. Everyone has a turn at being in the middle.

Make groups of not more than eight people. One person lies on the floor, eyes closed, the others stand at some distance. In silence, they approach the person on the floor and very gently raise them, cradle-like just off the level of the floor. They then see how they can move the person up and down with the minimum of effort and disturbance. The trust must not be broken and the exercise geared to the acceptance of the person being worked on. It is possible to raise the person to almost shoulder level and give everyone a shared responsibility for the safety of that person.

Mirrors

This very familiar exercise can prove to be destructive rather than constructive, if it is not executed properly. First, choose a partner. Decide who is to be the leader and call that person A, the one who is the mirror becomes B. The couple stand opposite each other, but not too close; they make eye contact, and that should be maintained all the time. A begins to move very slowly and easily, making sure that B is following the exact movements. It should appear as if no one is leading the exercise because the sensitivity between the two participants is of a high order. Allow no speech, and no attempt to trick your partner. There can be humour and wit, but not at the expense of sensitivity and harmony. At a given signal the partners change roles, at another signal no one leads. There could even be a moment when they close eyes for a while to see if the movements are still synchronized.

Do not stop the flow of movement when giving the next instruction. Explain the next move before indicating that it must happen. On a given signal they have to leave their partner and find another person to work with. The atmosphere of the room has to be maintained, and again no speaking is allowed as they assume either an active or submissive role. The exercise continues with the new partners.

A good variation can be to give the responsibility of changing partners to the group. This requires someone in the group to

Taped Music

Music can help some exercises but must be used with discretion. Tape the selected piece of music on a cassette and in some cases make repeats so that it can run for a long time. If you are confident with CDs, use them. Useful tracks are: Verdi's *Requiem, Offertorio*; Erik Satie; *Trios Gymnopedies*; Sibelius, *Swan of Tuonela*; *Tune and Air for Trumpet and Orchestra in D* by Purcell.

take the initiative and instigate the change. Again don't do this too early in the work, as it requires courage and good group awareness. This exercise allows you to observe the group as a whole and also to monitor individual reactions.

TAKING IT FURTHER

If all is going well, or on another occasion, add this variation. Get them working in pairs with the possible addition of music, something easy and soothing like the Satie. After one or two changes of partner then fade the music slightly and tell them to form groups of four. This will require them to rethink how they establish leadership and how this change will affect the way they move, for mirroring doesn't work. Let them solve the problem without interruption, but still respecting the atmosphere already established. Then, once they have settled, suggest two groups of eight, and finally, one group of sixteen. Allow them to continue with this for a while and if problems arise, let them try to solve them without interruption.

There will be lots of things to talk about, in the discussion that follows – for example – the person with whom you had an immediate rapport, the one who made you giggle, the one whose movements were difficult to follow and the one who couldn't look you in the eye.

The Elements

The following exercises look at the elements of earth, air, fire and water. Becoming something other than a human being is a good way of exploring qualities in a character, and also creating a specific environment when storytelling. Becoming the Gorgon Medusa or being the soldiers that Circe turns into pigs in the Odyssey, can be moments of wonderful theatre, and the transformation, accomplished by just using the actor's body, can be quite magical. To experience the elements also gives the actor some idea of how we, as humans, react to them. Do not attempt this exercise on the first day as it requires some physical contact, and until the actors have lost some of their inhibitions and are becoming happier with their own bodies, it is as well to stick with less challenging exercises.

Earth

Get the group to lie down on their backs with their knees raised, arms by their sides, palms upwards and eyes closed. This is called the *semi-supine position*. Get them to become aware of their breathing, and then start to play some music (the Satie, perhaps). The best way to start is for them to let their knees go, either to one side or the other. Once committed to movement they should imagine that their bodies are made of mercury, or without a skeleton, and just part of the floor. This means that they will eventually start to roll over the floor and encounter the other bodies. Let them discover how they deal with each other but still continue to explore the floor and their relationship with the space around them. This exercise can cause some disturbance, and that is perfectly in order as long as it is not trivial. If you feel they need support, fade the music and discuss, or give gentle instructions as they work.

Air

Having experienced the earth and then to become air immediately afterwards gives the actor a contrasting sensation from within. It starts with the actor standing, eyes either open or closed, but this time, when the music starts, they are floating without effort and completely supported by the air around them, like a cloud or a bird negotiating the thermals. Once committed to movement they cannot stop, but everything moves with great ease. Suggest that they think about where the impetus to move starts in the body. Encourage them to move in and around the other people, exploring the space, but without making contact.

An Anatomy Lesson

After discussing the exercise for what has been seen, felt and experienced, it can be beneficial to look at the actual weight of the human

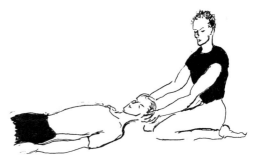

Taking the weight of the head.

Semi-supine position.

LEANING BACKWARDS

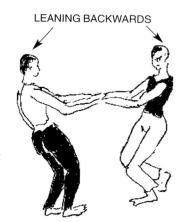

PUSHING
Back to Back
Sitting and Standing

TAKING YOUR PARTNER ON YOUR BACK

LYING BACK

on partners back

Sit in the small
of back

Squat

LEANING SIDEWAYS

Weight taking.

body. They will work in pairs, choosing someone about their own weight and size. One person lies on the floor in the semi-supine position; their partner kneels by their head, and without being helped lifts up the full weight of the partner's head in their hands. Likewise the pelvis is lifted. They discuss what they have discovered. This can be seen in terms of evolution. How we feel very much at home lying on the ground and its connection with rest and sleep. How muscle and sinew can make the body seem light or heavy without actually altering the weight. How by controlling static and dynamic tension we can create movements that have an expressive and dramatic power.

Weight Taking

Still working with the same partner, let them try taking each other's weight. Holding both hands and standing opposite each other let them bend their knees keeping an even balance between them. Once they get the hang of it they will find all kinds of variations, and it is also an excellent way of helping your partner have a good stretch.

Moulding Your Partner

Let them imagine that their partner is made of clay, and that they are a sculptor. It begins with one person being the lump of clay and the other being the sculptor. They begin to mould their partner into the statue of a person in a particular situation or emotional state. They could be a tennis champion serving a winning shot, or a mother grieving over her dead child. The clay person should be obedient to the touch of the sculptor and fulfil the demands made by the sculptor's hands. Once the work is complete, they change roles. The new sculptor makes a statue that relates to the first one.

We look at one pair at a time. They can choose where their sculpture should be in the room, and they do this whilst the rest of the participants close their eyes. The eyes are opened and we then see what impact the sculpture makes on the room and on us. As if we are in an art gallery we can view the sculpture from all angles. The pair must retain stillness and integrity. The viewers can voice what they see and what they think the story behind the statue is. Many scenarios develop, and not always those intended by the creators. Make sure that the comments are clear and that the observations are precise, for example: 'The way he is pointing his finger at her tells me . . .'.

Water

Imaging

Start the exercise in the semi-supine position with eyes closed. Begin to play *The Swan of Tuonela*, and as they listen get them to imagine that they are floating on a large lake or river. Fill their imaginations with the feeling of the water under them, of the sunlight coming through the trees, of the gentle current helping them down the river. They are now in the river, below the surface, and can see and move about among the life of the river that is now all around them. Still below the surface they drift out to sea. They are now surrounded by coral and seaweed, huge ray fish, shoals of smaller coloured fish, and the life on the ocean bed. Bring them back to the surface and land them on a sandy beach, and then back to the room. The eyes are then opened, but this time without discussion we move into the next phase of the exercise.

From Fish Bowl to Seabed

Divide them into groups of four or five people. Place them around the room, so that they are not too close together. Using just their hands instruct them to create an aquarium, or fish tank. They can become the reeds and rocks,

How groups can use the space.

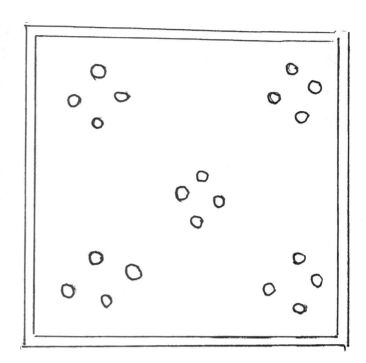

the fish, the crabs and sea anemones, any creature that they want. If they don't 'like' what they are creating, they can create another creature or plant.

Start with stillness and silence, and make sure you have both. Then start to play the same music again and watch. This is a good time for you to observe individuals. Allow them time to establish their world and to play. Fade the music. Allow only a brief discussion, do not destroy the atmosphere.

They are now going to bring their whole bodies into the exercise. It starts as before, with just the hands, they then begin to transform using the whole body and also the whole of the room. Groups can now merge. Shoals of fish can dash around the seabed. Coral reefs can appear and disappear. Once this instruction has been understood, silence and stillness is requested and the music starts again. They may need encouragement but be patient, for

an underwater world will appear before your eyes that you will be tempted to join. (This is possible if done discreetly and also can help develop the exercise.) When you think they have had enough, encourage them to return to their groups and let the movements become smaller until they end up working with their hands only.

A good discussion should follow. There are lots of things to talk about – becoming something or someone other than yourself, seeing and believing in the world you can create, allowing the whole body to be involved, and most importantly there is the constant desire to tell stories and develop relationships and scenarios even if you are a fish or a rock or a strand of seaweed. Also how you are affected by your environment.

Fire

Exploring the element of fire can begin in a

33

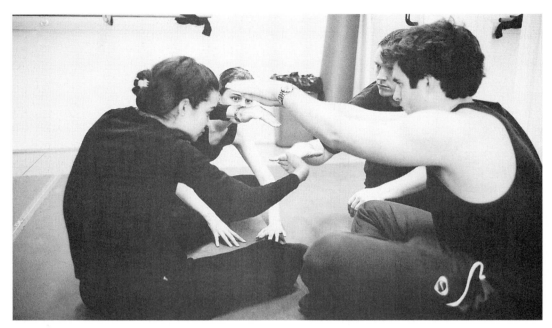

Creating an aquarium with the hands. Photo: Alan Boyle

Becoming the creatures. Photo: Alan Boyle

Taking it into the body. Photos: Alan Boyle

similar way to water with the company working in small groups. Using only their hands they will create a small bonfire. Suggest they create the sounds of the fire with their voices. Let them discover what will increase the intensity of the fire. What it is that starts a fire in nature, like the sun's rays burning a dried leaf or twig, and then the wind increasing the heat and spreading the fire. Suggest that the small bonfires begin to spread so that eventually the whole room is like an inferno.

Combining the Elements into an Improvisation

Choose a suitable piece of music – for example, something from *The Planets* by Holst or the *Hebrides Overture* by Mendelssohn, for them to work to. Have equal groups for earth, fire, water and air, and place them about the space so they are separated from each other. The drama begins when the music starts. Earth emerges out of the sea, vegetation appears, trees and grass begin to grow on the land. The sun (fire) first helps the trees to grow and then as the leaves dry the sun's heat starts a fire. The waves come and extinguish the flames and the fire turns to steam. The battle of the elements – lightning, rain, flood and drought – can all be created, in a continuous dance drama. See if they can find some resolution to the improvisation.

STATUS

It is important for the actor to have an understanding of status. This not only applies to where a role they might be playing stands in the hierarchy of the play, but also how in life they as individuals are perceived and how they perceive themselves. To take an example, how does the body react when the character they might be playing is suddenly crowned King.

The following exercise can be played with any age group and is usually enjoyed by all. Let us assume you are working with a group of sixteen actors. Ask them what they understand by the term status. In the conversation that follows, you could draw examples from well-known plays to point out how important status is when creating a character. Finally, make a clear definition so that the exercise can proceed easily, and tell them that their status will be donated by a number. The highest number carries with it the highest status, and is the King or Emperor, the lowest number is the slave, beggar, or down-and-out.

You should have prepared eight pieces of paper on which is clearly written the numbers one to eight. (If you need more numbers make sure that you make a mark on the nine or six to avoid confusion.) Fold the numbered pieces of paper and place them in an envelope.

The group choose partners, A and B. All the As choose a number without showing it to anyone else, memorize it and return the piece of paper to you. The Bs are asked to observe, not only the whole group, but to pay particular attention to the way in which their partner goes about the exercise.

The exercise begins with all the participants standing round the edge of the room facing the wall. During the exercise they cannot speak or touch another member of the group. They take on their number's status in the way that they contact the others and how they carry themselves physically. The exercise commences when the room is quiet. They then turn to face each other. They are free to move about the room, and once they feel that they know every one else's number they will fall still. Be warned this can take some time. The first part of the exercise is now over.

One of the viewers volunteers to put the participants in order of status. They should remain in their roles as they are being moved so they can express how they feel at being put in the wrong position for their status. This also

Large Groups

If you are working with large groups of actors divide them up into teams or subgroups so that an exercise can be watched. In such cases, they will not need to make any preparation. They just listen and learn from the previous group's improvisation, and apply what has been seen and learnt to their own work. If you are working with younger students or those you haven't worked with before, it can help to have some older, more experienced students to lead the groups, help to keep the focus, and develop the exercise from within.

Watching each other working. Guildford students in a travelling exercise.
Photo: Alan Boyle

gives the one who is grading them some more clues as to their status, but they are only given one chance to get it right. Another viewer volunteers to change the order. One of the participants can be asked if they are happy where they have been placed. If not they can assume their correct position. Eventually when you think the line is correct, the numbers are called out.

Observations are made by the watchers, and the experience discussed by the participants. The watchers, taking on what they have seen and heard, are now given the chance to choose a number and the process is repeated. We have thus established a way of learning through watching and then doing.

VARIATIONS

You can play a number of variations. To do this you will have to prepare some more envelopes. One will have all fours and fives, another lots of sevens and eights and a single one, another with lots of ones and twos and just one eight. At first the group is very confused, but once they realize that you are playing with them, they engage with enthusiasm.

In this way the exercise can turn into an improvisation. For instance, with the last suggestion you immediately create a prisoner-of-war camp, or an exercise yard in a gaol being watched over by a single guard. Allow them to develop the improvisation with the addition of speech.

THE FOUR SEASONS

The following exercise works very well at the end of a morning or afternoon session, when they have been working with each other and getting used to physical contact. They have explored many ways of using their bodies, and now need to find some individuality and also get used to working on their own in small groups of four or five people per group. The first direction is to create a tableau entitled 'The Four Seasons'. There can be

Sheffield Youth Theatre creating a tableau.

38

Giving Directions

When giving a series of directions to actors make sure first that they are still and concentrating on what you say. Then ask if there are any questions. If there are none, tell them to move into position and wait in silence for the signal to start. If there are queries do not repeat yourself, but allow another member of the group to explain the direction. Don't let giving directions end up in a discussion. You do not know what is going to happen, once the exercise or scene starts.

times when the tableau moves, which allows them to create the four seasons, to create moments of stillness and also to experience transforming from one season to another. It should be viewed from all angles, like a monument in a public square or garden. Allow them about fifteen minutes to work together. Keep the time short which stops too much discussion and promotes action. If one group is not trying things out give them a nudge.

Once they have created something let them try it out, but do not let them become too involved in fixing every move and detail. We now come to sharing the work. Number the groups so they know in which order they are to perform their tableaux. The groups disperse

A post-exercise discussion.

themselves around the room so they are not next to anyone in their group, but opposite them. Without discussion they are directed to find some way of entering the space before forming their tableau and once they arrive at the final pose to stay still and fixed until the next group moves in to replace them. Once they are released, they move out of the central area and back to the edges of the studio to watch the next group perform their tableau. The direction to begin will come when the music starts (use the Offertorio from Verdi's *Requiem*).

The discussion that follows will produce lots of interesting observations and the potential of togetherness and group responsibility that the exercise creates will give you a good idea about the group as a whole. These exercises can be incorporated into your rehearsal period if you think that they are appropriate to the material you will be working on. The essential function of the exercises and games in this chapter is for the release of imagination and for freedom from inhibition. The later work of rehearsal is geared towards performance and is therefore more rigorous and critical.

3 CHOOSING MATERIAL

This can be one of the most crucial decisions that you will need to take when embarking upon a youth theatre production. It is important that you respect the piece of work, and that you feel inspired by the writing, the story and the characters, so that it will bring out the best in you. But what *you* might like as a play or musical may not be to the liking of your audience or your troupe of young actors. Enthusiasm and belief in the product is essential, in order for you, your cast and crew, to communicate in the fullest way the intentions of the playwright.

In this chapter I am going to make some suggestions of plays that I know have been successfully performed by young casts, and that also offer the opportunity to include large numbers of actors. Your youth theatre may have a large membership, so you will want to include as many members as possible. Before we look at particular plays, let us consider some pointers to help assess a play that would be suitable for production.

Copyright and Royalties

Nearly all published writing is held in copyright for at least fifty years after the death of the author. If you want to perform a published play you must get the permission of the playwright, and in most cases be subject to a royalty fee. In the front of the copy of the play or book you will find the name of the person to whom you have to apply for permission. You will have to abide by the wishes of the author, and not make any alterations to the text without their permission. The same applies to literary work and music. Before you advertise your event make sure that you have the rights to do it. Translations of foreign plays are also subject to royalties.

LANGUAGE

Be aware of the convention in which the play is written. For instance, Shakespeare can be performed very successfully by a youth theatre but you cannot expect the young actors to be able to sight-read it at will. They might never have seen a play before, let alone one written in iambic pentameter, so it is likely that they may initially be intimidated by the complexity of the syntax, and the unusual vocabulary. If you choose a Shakespeare you will need to find an original and inventive way into the play during the early stages of rehearsal.

With *Zigger Zagger* by Peter Terson, which was commissioned for the National Youth Theatre, you will have no problems. It contains strong but not offensive language, and because it was written for the actors and is about their world, it communicates in a heightened form using their own way of speaking. *Road* by Jim Cartwright could be considered a suitable vehicle for older youth theatre actors but it does contain strong language and could cause problems with parents, members of staff, and of course your audience.

My Fair Lady, the musical version of *Pygmalion*, needs a Higgins who can cope with those long Shavian sentences that even experienced professionals find hard to deliver, whereas *Joseph and his Amazing Technicolour Dreamcoat* was originally written for schoolchildren to perform and presents no problems.

CONTENT

Choose a good story that is told through action rather than reflection. It doesn't matter if there are lots of scenes as long as they are not too long and advance the action. Beware of plays that deal with contemporary issues that expose the actors to explicit scenes of violence, sexuality and extreme social problems in a crude and unimaginative way. The young actor will often want to explore these issues out of curiosity, fear, or a need to be understood, but unless such plays are expertly written, it is best to keep these explorations to the rehearsal room.

Historical documentaries make good subjects for young performers, but to develop this form of theatre you will need the assistance and skill of a writer/editor, but there are in existence a number of texts. There are many way in which you can gather material, from verbatim reports on tape recorders, to historical documents and maps. Also the great Victorian novelists, like Wilkie Collins, the Brontë sisters and Charles Dickens are open to adaptation, and if you do your own there is, of course, no royalty involved.

CHARACTER

If the play is explored with intelligence and skill it is amazing how convincing young actors can be in the roles of characters many years their senior. However, it is the spirit of youth that needs to be tapped in youth theatre, a simple directness of communication of the truth rather than a poor imitation of adult behaviour, and a stereotypical approach to character. It is best to avoid the European naturalistic plays of the late nineteenth and early twentieth centuries, such as Gorky, Chekhov and Ibsen (with the exception of *Peer Gynt*), with characters of psychological complexity and hidden symbolism. To attempt Greek tragedy could cause problems with a young actor having to interpret and sustain the character of Medea. However, an older member could be cast as the central character, but for a youth theatre to interpret the comedies of Aristophanes or of the Roman playwright Plautus could prove a stimulating and highly entertaining event.

POSSIBLE PLAYS

The Frogs by Aristophanes

This is a comedy concerning Dionysus and his journey into Hades to bring back the poet who will save the city from ruin. There are thirteen named characters and lots of work for the chorus. It offers plenty of opportunity for original music and imaginative design. You will find it in a translation by David Barrett published by Penguin Classics, or in a translation by Kenneth McLeish published by Methuen Drama in *Aristophanes Plays 2*.

The Chester Mystery Plays

This is an adaptation of the plays that were presented by the craft guilds. The four major cycles hail from Chester, York, Wakefield and the so-called Coventry plays that were performed throughout the city on carts until the reign of Elizabeth I who put a stop to the mystery plays but allowed the morality plays to be performed. They have big casts and offer many different opportunities for performance, for instance in a church as a promenade production, in the open air or conventionally on a stage. It is in print in a version by Heinemann as *The Chester Mystery Plays* adapted into Modern English by Maurice Hussey.

The Mysteries

Tony Harrison's version of the mystery plays is a fresh, vital and poetic adaptation that was used in Bill Bryden's production for the Cottesloe Theatre in London. This is in print by Faber and Faber. It also has a big cast and similar scope to the above version.

The *Odyssey*

The stage version of Homer's epic by Derek Walcott, the West Indian poet, was originally performed by a mixed-race cast of seventeen at the Royal Shakespeare Company. It could encompass a larger cast, and is printed by Faber and Faber.

SOME PLAYS BY SHAKESPEARE

A Midsummer Night's Dream

This is a good choice for a young company. It would require clever cutting and an imaginative approach if it is to be considered for an inexperienced youth theatre. There are some good leading roles but it is definitely a company piece.

As You Like It

Like the *Dream* this play has a lot of good parts and a fast-moving plot that is easy to follow. A lot of the text is in prose which presents less of a problem with verse speaking, but it does require a really able actor for Rosalind. It is a good play to choose for an all-male or all-female cast.

Twelfth Night

Set in Illyria, the story concerns the adventures of twins Viola and Sebastian who are separated in a terrible sea storm until they are finally reunited and find love and romance in marriage (not to each other!). There are many rich characters, like Sir Toby Belch, Sir

A Midsummer Night's Dream *rehearsal.*

Andrew Ague-cheek, Maria, Malvolio, Olivia and Feste.

The Comedy of Errors

This is a beautifully constructed comedy that needs lots of energy in performance and has a good sense of fun. The director would need to feel at home with the conventions of comedy and farce, without losing the very strong story line.

The Taming of the Shrew

Like the previous play this has lots of fun characters and a strong plot. With imagination it can accommodate a large cast that includes wedding guests and Petruchio's servants. Bear in mind that this play is quite long so that expert cutting would be an important requirement before embarking on it.

The Tempest (Sheffield Youth Theatre).

All's Well That Ends Well

This is a complex play with interesting parts for the girls, and contains a mixture of comedy and drama that has a fantastical element to it. I have seen it performed with a cast of about twenty actors aged from twelve or thirteen to twenty years old, with many of the roles double cast.

The Tempest

Considered to be one of Shakespeare's most complex plays, and thought to be his last, this is a favourite with Youth Theatres. It lends

The Tempest (A&BC Theatre). Helium balloon and oil-drum setting at the Volgograd Boat Station.

The same production beneath a Saman Tree in Trinidad.

itself well to being performed alfresco, and because of the magical quality of the writing can have more than one actor playing Prospero and Ariel.

PLAYS WITH LARGE CASTS THAT ARE SET IN A SPECIFIC PLACE

The Rimers of Eldritch

The story, by Lanford Wilson, revolves around a Mid-West Community in the United States. Skelly, an eccentric recluse, is shot in the woods by a middle-aged spinster. The story is told through a series of flashbacks that eventually reveal the truth behind the killing. This is a true company piece that needs a certain maturity of character from the actors, and a skilful approach from the director. It is written to be performed with the minimum of costume and set, and ideally no props. It has a cast of seventeen (ten women and seven men). Published by Spotlight Dramabook, Hill and Wang, New York.

Our Town

This is Thornton Wilder's classic about a small-town community and told in a similar but less complex way than *The Rimers of Eldritch*. This play has one huge part for the Stage Manager, and a skilled and mature challenge for the rest of the cast. It has twenty-two named characters and a simple versatile setting. It is printed by Longmans, Green and Co., and entitled *Three Plays by Thornton Wilder*.

Under Milk Wood by Dylan Thomas

Originally written for radio, the play responds well to many approaches, from a small, versatile group of actors to a large cast. It needs a real flavour of the Welsh accent to be truly successful and has some wonderful characters and wit. The First Voice, like the Stage Manager in *Our Town*, is a massive part but the responsibility can be shared by a few people if necessary.

Our Day Out by Willy Russell

This is a play with songs that started life as a television production but has been adapted very successfully by the author to the stage. It does require five adult players for the play to work, but could be useful in a school where staff/student relationships are good or need strengthening. The songs are easy to learn and tuneful, and the design needs careful

Prospero silhouetted against the helium moon.

Under Milk Wood *with GSA students in Captain Cat's dream.*

45

Under Milk Wood *at GSA – Polly Garter's song. Photo by Mark Dean, setting by Barry Jarvis.*

consideration but it could be done very simply. The places that the school trip visits are important and need to be considered when choosing the play.

Zigger Zagger by Peter Terson

This was specially commissioned by The National Youth Theatre of Great Britain in the early 1960s and was very successful. It is now slightly dated but could be treated as a period piece. Football mania and the problems of becoming an adult in present-day urban society is still relevant and worth exploring. It's a good vigorous text with lots of opportunities for actors and can accommodate a huge cast.

Zigger Zagger is printed by Penguin modern playwrights with *Mooney and His Caravans*. There is a good preface by Michael Croft, who commissioned the play and was its first director, which diaries the first production.

Peer Gynt by Henrik Ibsen, translated by Kenneth McLeish

There are forty-seven named parts in this adaptation including three Peers. This is a good translation that will need to be cut to meet the requirements of a Youth Theatre, but it has some wonderful scenes and a good story with lots of reference points for a young audience and cast.

The Caucasian Chalk Circle by Bertolt Brecht

This version is translated by James and Tania Stern with W.H. Auden and published by Methuen Drama. An epic tale based on an old Chinese legend is performed by some travelling players before members of two villages, as they debate what will happen to the valley now the war is over. The play can survive without the prologue, and offers opportunities for original presentation, but if you are a purist then you will be compelled to do the whole play. A huge cast makes it a suitable choice for a big company with strong leading roles, and again has opportunities for singing and music. The story is immense with battle scenes, escapes across collapsing rope bridges, a huge trial and a tender story of love and loyalty. Again you may have to trim the text to your needs, but do it carefully.

The Fat Prince's mask designed by Russell Dean for GSA's production of The Caucasian Chalk Circle.

The Governor Georgi Abashvili's mask for the same production.

ADAPTATION

The *Mahabharata* by Jean Claude Carrière, translated by Peter Brook

There are three plays in the adaptation performed originally by Peter Brook's multiracial company all over the world. It offers scope and imagination to the cast and company, and can be performed almost anywhere. These plays present a good opportunity for ensemble playing and music. It is printed in Great Britain by Cox and Wyman, published by Methuen London, 11 New Fetter Lane, London EC4P 4EE.

A Christmas Carol, adapted by John Mortimer

Dickens's brilliant look at a Victorian Christmas has been dramatized with sixty named parts and a chorus offering a wonderful alternative to the seasonal pantomime. Songs and carols intersperse the action and there is imaginative scope for the director and designer. This version, and there are quite a few, is published by Samuel French who also hold the rights.

Nicholas Nickleby

Offering wonderful opportunities for everyone concerned, this is a two-part adaptation by David Edgar that has a huge cast. Originally commissioned by the Royal Shakespeare Company, it has been performed in many countries and more recently with much success by the National Youth Theatre.

MUSICAL

With the popularity of the modern musical there is a huge choice on offer. Many of the works of Lloyd-Webber are still being performed, so obtaining the rights could cause problems. Many of them are sung through – that is, they have no book like *My Fair Lady*, so it is difficult to get an idea of what they are like unless you read music. They can also be expensive to mount because you will need to hire scores as well as scripts, and they demand a high standard of production. Do not let this deter you, but make sure you have a cast that is able to sing the score, and that you have an experienced Musical Director to teach the music and keep the singing voices in good trim.

If you are considering mounting a musical, try and get hold of a copy of *The Book of*

Musical Theatre terminology

There are certain terms used in musical theatre that you may not be familiar with. 'Sung Through' means there is no spoken dialogue – the whole story is told through song; 'Book' means the spoken text of the musical; 'Lyrics' means the words of the song: 'Choreography' means the dances. Some musicals have all these aspects of the production under copyright which might mean you will need everybody's permission before you can go ahead.

Musical Theatre by Ganzl. It is published by Bodley Head and covers all the musical shows presented in the United Kingdom, the United States of America, France and Germany from the late nineteenth century until the present day. It contains the main characters, the authors, choreographers and composers, original casts and a detailed synopsis of the story. The following list might give you some ideas but it is only a fraction of the musicals covered in this book. If you want to get an idea of the score and the demands it will put on the young performer you will find the most well-known musicals have been recorded on CD or tape, so either borrow a copy from your local library or buy one. Just remember that for a musical to work you will need good strong singing voices, that can survive the rigours of rehearsals and performances.

The Beggar's Opera

The 'First Musical' written by John Gay with music selected and arranged by Johann Pepusch in the eighteenth century, and a cast of eleven men and eight women plus others proves to be a rousing and entertaining play. The songs are beautiful and demand to be sung, but with a pure simplicity. The characters are clearly drawn and are full of the vibrancy of low-life London.

The Operettas of Gilbert and Sullivan

There are at least a dozen of these very popular operettas with witty lyrics, complex choruses, operatic arias and well crafted books. The principal characters all need good singing voices to deal with the clever but quite complex scores.

The Boy Friend

This is a very successful pastiche of the twenties musical with songs and lyrics by Sandy Wilson, who also wrote the book. It has a cast of nine women and ten men and takes place in a finishing school in Nice for 'Perfect Young Ladies'. This musical offers a tuneful score and an opportunity for clever choreography, but it needs a stylish, witty production.

Salad Days

This opened in London at the same time as *The Boy Friend* and is a romantic fantasy about university graduates and a magical piano that sets people dancing. With music by Julian Slade and book and lyrics by Dorothy Reynolds, it is a series of witty sketches linked by a charming but slight romance, and a simple, very pretty score.

Oliver

Oliver has seven women and nine named male roles, but there can be a huge cast to bring to life Victorian London, and Fagin's Den with his band of young pickpockets. It has great songs, vibrant characters and of course a marvellously gripping story. The book and the lyrics are by Lionel Bart and, of course, Charles Dickens.

Half a Sixpence

This has a book by Beverly Cross from the novel *Kipps* by H.G. Wells and music and lyrics by David Heneker. It was originally performed by Tommy Steele and had a successful run at the London Palladium.

Joseph and his Amazing Technicolour Dreamcoat

This is a rock opera by Tim Rice with music by Andrew Lloyd-Webber. The story is taken from the Old Testament. Joseph is a 'sung through' musical, and was originally written to be performed by a school. It has a predominance of male characters with fifteen named male characters and only one female.

Jesus Christ Superstar

This is another rock opera by the same team, with nine men and only one named female character, Mary Magdalen. It tells the story of the crucifixion of Christ and is again 'sung through'. There are lots of good chorus numbers but care must be taken in casting the lead roles as the vocal demands and conventions used by the creators can put enormous strains on a young, untrained voice.

Godspell

This is another rock opera based on the Gospel according to St Matthew, by John Michael Teblak with music by Stephen Schwartz. It was very popular in the 1960s and 1970s and was originally performed by a cast of ten.

Guys and Dolls

This is based on a novel by Damon Runyon and Jo Swerling lyrics and music by Frank Loesser, and tells the story of a romance between a Salvation Army girl and a gangster. It has some wonderful songs and energy, but needs money, inventive choreography, good accents and strong direction.

Grease

This is a rock and roll musical by Jim Jacobs and Warren Casey that is very popular with young performers and audiences. It has seventeen named parts and makes a good company show. There is also a very successful film that is available on video.

The Rocky Horror Show by Richard O'Brien

This is a great favourite with young audiences and young performers. This musical will need careful marketing so as not to offend the older and straight-laced members of the community.

Billy Liar

This is a musical play by Keith Waterhouse and Willis Hall with music by Ian La Fresnais and Dick Clement from the play *Billy Liar*. Set in Lancashire the story concerns Billy, a north country Walter Mitty, and inveterate liar, and his romantic entanglements with three young women. Both play and musical are good-humoured, and written with an acute sense of character.

Blood Brothers

A very successful musical about two brothers brought up by a different set of parents, with book, lyrics and music by Willy Russell. It has three wonderful parts for the two boys and the mother, and the songs are tuneful and not too difficult.

CREATING YOUR OWN SHOW

You may decide that none of the plays you have looked at are right for your company and that you would like to create your own piece of theatre. If you have done this before, the following suggestions may be familiar; however, it is important to be aware of some fundamental facts. To pursue in detail how to devise and write would make a book in itself. However, here are a few pointers to help you on your way.

Galahad *poster.*

THE HISTORICAL DOCUMENTARY

There are various historical documentaries that were created in the 1960s and 70s both in the UK and North America: *The Stirrings in Sheffield, a Musical* documentary which was about the Grinders, and *The Roses of Eyham* that was about how the Great Plague came to a Derbyshire village. Ensemble pieces about The Expo Olympics, and the Depression of the 1930s were developed by George Luscombe in Canada using a lot of verbatim material. *Rural Rides* by William Cobbett has been used as a basis for a play about the plight of the farm labourer in Wiltshire during the early nineteenth century. Your district may have some gems of local history that are well documented and offer good dramatic possibilities, but transferring these into a play can prove a tricky exercise.

THE ADAPTED NOVEL

Some very distinguished playwrights have successfully adapted the novels of the Victorian era. An epic poem like Longfellow's *Hiawatha* has a good potential for dramatization. It offers a strong story and some beautiful language that can then be mixed in with some Native American creation myths and tales.

DEVISING

This is a slow process and one that some members may find too demanding, but with careful preparation and research it can prove to be very rewarding. Timeless age-old stories offer a wonderful opportunity for storytelling. The process of creation and performance blends into one. Whether your source material is from works of the Brothers Grimm, Hans Christian Andersen, The Bible or some ancient Indian Creation Myths, you can engage a young company's imagination and expertise in the simplest and most direct form of theatre, and get them to tell the story in their own way without diverging from its truth and integrity.

There is a whole chapter dedicated to the devising process but remember you might need the assistance of a writer/editor. However, in choosing someone, make sure they are of a generous and sensitive nature and will be prepared to listen to and reflect the company's voice and written contributions.

Every piece of theatre puts a different demand upon everyone concerned, but as you work and begin to increase your repertoire of plays so you will find a common approach to presentation, and Chapter 5 will give you some idea about how your production will look, and also offer you some alternatives about how the actors can develop new relationships with their audience. Before we explore that, let us now look at the preparation you will need to make before you start rehearsal, not only artistic decisions but practical arrangements that can free you so that you can devote your time and energy to working with your actors.

4 PRE-REHEARSAL PLANNING

In this chapter we will look at what needs to be done once you have chosen your play and your company of actors. Your tasks can be divided into two categories. First there are practical decisions to be made to which you will need to know the answers, and these are informed by the artistic and creative research and preparation you will need to do on the text, assuming that you are preparing to direct an established play.

READING THE PLAY

Before casting the play you will have read it a number of times to get an idea of the characters and how you see them being realized by the actors. You will now need to know more facts about the play. To do this it is useful to make specific lists. The first one to consider is:

* **The epic world of the play.** Our search is to find out where and when the play takes place and to explore the atmosphere of the time and the different environments. Write down your discoveries so that you can refer to that information at a glance. Then, there will be the stage directions. These could have been written by the author, but some may have been added by an editor to make it easier reading or taken from the original prompt copy. So use your discretion as to

how valid they are. The internal directions can be easily overlooked, especially when the facts are contained within the dialogue. Scene by scene you will begin to gather this vital information about the play that will inform you about the artistic liberties you may wish to take in updating or altering that epic world, for example setting *Hamlet* in a mental institution rather than the royal castle in Elsinore.

* **The dramatic world of the play** is the action of the story, that is, the dramatic line, what happens and to whom. You will need to find out where the climaxes to the story occur and the emotional changes and decisions that the characters have to make in order to survive and achieve their own desires and objectives, and how these decisions affect the development of the story. Be careful in making this investigation that you are clear about what is explicit and what is implicit in the text. At the moment we are only dealing with facts.

* **Dividing the play into scenes and units**. Some plays are already divided up into scenes, like the plays from the Elizabethan era. Bertolt Brecht always gives a title or introduction to each scene, and it is a useful practice for you to do the same. This will not only help you to see how the action is developing but it also aids the rehearsal process. An obvious place is when a new

The Winters' Tale

ACT I	PLACE	CHARACTERS	HEADING
SCENE I	Sicilia	Camillo Archidamus	The Lords discuss their masters
SCENE II	Sicilia	Leontes Politenes Camillo Mamillius Hermione	Jealousy
ACT II			
SCENE I	Sicilia	Leontes Antigonus Lord Mamillius Hermione 1st & 2nd Lady	Hermione jailed for for infidelity
SCENE II	Sicilia Outside Jail	Gaoler A genetleman Paulina Emilia	The Birth of Perdita
SCENE III	Sicilia Leontes Chamber	Leontes Antigonus Lord Paulina Two servants	The Baby Perdita to be exiled and abandoned

The Winter's Tale, *early breakdown of scenes and characters.*

character or characters enter the scene, but a new unit can occur when some vital information is revealed by a character, or the action suddenly changes direction because of a character's reaction to the situation. Once you start working with the actors they will need guidance and discipline to help them make crucial decisions about their characters. It is better to decide with them on the units rather than impose personal decisions about the look and interpretation of the play before the actors have started their work for this could remove any opportunity for them to bring their own discoveries to the production.

To understand this process in more detail let us look at the first scene in *A Midsummer Night's Dream*. If we just take the initial stage directions and the first speech of Theseus, let us see what we discover.

ACT ONE

Scene 1 Athens, the palace of Theseus
Enter Theseus, Hipployta, Philostrate
and Attendants.
Theseus: Now, fair Hippolyta, our nuptial
hour
Draws on apace; four happy days
bring in
Another moon; but, O, methinks,
how slow
This old moon wanes! She lingers
my desires,
Like to a step-dame or a dowager,
Long withering out a young man's
revenue.

First let us consider the epic world. The place is the palace of Theseus who we learn from the Dramatis Personae is the Duke of Athens. His bride-to-be Hippolyta is Queen of the Amazons, and it is four days before the next new moon. The dramatic action is, that although Theseus is very happy about becoming Hippolyta's husband he is impatient to be married, 'but, O methinks, how slow this old moon wanes! She lingers my desires. . .'. There follows a short loving exchange between Hippolyta and Theseus that is interrupted by Egeus's entrance. This completes the first unit that could be entitled 'Happy marriage arrangements'. The next unit brings a whole new story into the play, and could be entitled, 'A complaining father'. By this practical examination of a text we begin to discover what the play is saying, not what we imagine it is saying. All these investigations will inform how we approach the play and interpret it. This examination of the text will inevitably lead us on to do some research

Research

To fully understand what is being said it becomes important to delve into the world of Greek mythology which Shakespeare would have known about because in those days children were classically educated. You may be lucky and have studied Greek and Roman mythology, but your young actors may know nothing about it. Find the simplest and most attractive way of answering their question when they begin to study the play for performance. Shakespeare is possibly an extreme case for research but all plays are about special and different worlds, and to do justice to them does require investigation of one kind or another. A good dictionary is essential when dealing with Shakespeare, and also an edition of the text with useful and comprehensive notes. The Arden series, Penguin, and Applause first folio editions, which not only contain the original punctuation, but also a blank page opposite the text for your own notes, are helpful as are any other reference books that are relevant to the play's characters or period.

PREPARATION FOR FORMAL MEETINGS

You are now ready to have some formalized meetings that will involve the other members of your team. It would be a good idea to acquaint yourself with the glossary of theatrical terms on p. 150. It will help you when coming in contact with your local theatre or a specialist you have hired to enhance some aspect of your production. It will also help in creating a universal language with which to communicate with the rest of the company.

PRODUCTION MEETINGS

If your Youth Theatre company is connected with a school or college it will be much easier for you to have informal meetings with possible collaborators. Possibilities include a

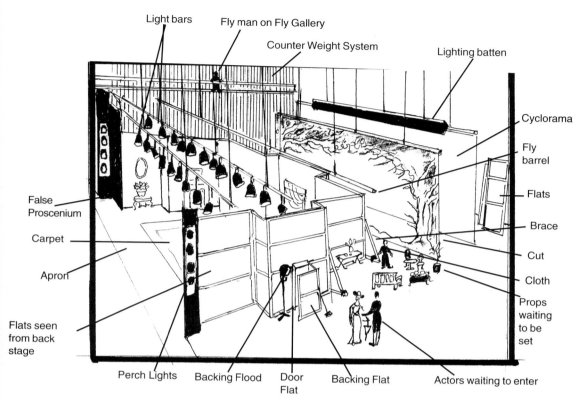

Light bars
Fly man on Fly Gallery
Counter Weight System
Lighting batten
Cyclorama
Fly barrel
Flats
Brace
Cut
Cloth
Props waiting to be set
False Proscenium
Carpet
Apron
Flats seen from back stage
Perch Lights
Backing Flood
Door Flat
Backing Flat
Actors waiting to enter

A look backstage at a conventional theatre.

drink in the pub after schooltime with your designer who has had some fresh ideas or a group of students who would like to be involved on the technical side, but these conversations have to be formalized. Before the rehearsals start, a number of more formal meetings have to be arranged. If your company is an independent organization that is relying on your local theatre for support, you will have to be well prepared before you meet up with the following.

The Manager or Director of the Professional Theatre, Arts Centre or Venue

This will be a professionally appointed position. If he has invited you into his venue he will need to know all about your production, the setting, the publicity hand-outs, the size of the company, the printing of tickets, and he will want you to sign some kind of contract or agreement. He will have the following on his staff:

A Press and Publicity Officer

This person will be responsible for advertising the list of plays and entertainments that the venue will be hosting for the season. The Press Officer will want to know about your posters, and will also be looking for ways in which to advertise your play, especially in their brochure. Youth theatre does have a particular local interest and the Press Department will want to know facts about the production that can be used for advertising your play. A word of warning, however – do not promise anything you cannot deliver, and remember to protect your company from any negative publicity.

The Production Manager/Stage Director

This person will want to know all about the technical demands of your production, the setting, the lighting design, the sound needed, whether you will have an orchestra, if you are using the audience for entrances. There will a resident backstage staff but you might have to supply extra people, so it could give some of your young technicians the chance to learn from professionals. You need to make a good friend of this person. He will let you know about the dangers of working in a professional set-up, and the risks involved in working in a professional theatre, and what would be the possible involvement of your own technicians.

THE YOUTH THEATRE

As you are not a professional company it is not imperative for you to fulfil all the roles that a professional company carries, but it is important that you know what these roles are, and it will help you to know who should be present at the various production meetings you will need to arrange.

Backstage Etiquette

Young people get very excited on their first visit, and being backstage invites exploration, but the place is filled with dangers and the space has to be treated with respect and caution. If your company makes a bad impression they may not be invited back.

The Producer

This is the person who gathers together all the talents and is responsible for the financial aspects of the production, that is, raising money and investigating the possibility of funding from local arts bodies and councils.

The Director

This is the person who is responsible for the artistic quality of the production. He or she works with the following:

The Designer

The Designer creates the sets and costumes. The job involves making working drawings, a ground plan and also a scale model of the set. The Designer will work very closely with the following:

The Carpenter

The Carpenter is responsible for building the scenery. In your company it might be the same person as the designer.

The Wardrobe Mistress

The Wardrobe Mistress will interpret the designer's drawings, and be responsible for seeing that everyone is appropriately dressed. The wardrobe department will often take on the task of designing and making the costumes. It is wise to make sure all those costumes that have survived the last production are cleaned and stored. Large casts mean there have to be many costumes, and this can become a very expensive item. A basic costume provided by each member of the company can help to alleviate the problem. A simple drawing and list can easily be provided by the wardrobe department and either circulated to cast members by post or at the first rehearsal.

A Lighting and Sound Designer

In recent years, as technology has advanced so has the lighting of plays and musicals. Young people are quick to pick up the way in which sophisticated equipment operates and though it means yet another person to accommodate in the production, it helps to build an involved and efficient technical team.

THE STAGE MANAGEMENT TEAM

A good, efficient and friendly stage management team is essential to the success of any production whether professional, amateur or youth theatre. It is through the stage management that all the aspects of the production pass. Its prime function is the ability to communicate with everybody. They pacify the temperamental actor and the harassed wardrobe mistress. They make friends with local traders who will lend valuable props free of charge and they make sure that everybody turns up on time knowing what scene they are expected to rehearse.

The Stage Manager

The Stage Manager heads the team and his or her immediate boss is the Production Manager. In an ideal situation the Stage Manager should be able to move from one department to another and to oversee and organize the team.

The Deputy Stage Manager or DSM

This is the Director's personal assistant, and is responsible for keeping the book up to date, for calling the actors and seeing that they arrive on time, making notes about the changes in props, and costumes, and getting details of forthcoming rehearsals. The DSM arrives before rehearsal starts and never leaves the rehearsal room until everyone has left.

Once the play is in performance the DSM runs the show from the prompt corner, giving the cues to the lighting board, the flies and sound, and getting the audience into their seats so that the play can go up on time.

Prompt Copy or Book

A record of the production is kept by the DSM. The text of the play is interleaved with blank pages, and all the movements of the actors and the placing of furniture is recorded in the book. These may alter during rehearsals, but once the play is in performance they should all be set down. All the calls are marked in for the actors' entrances, the sound cues, the lighting cues, the flies and tab's cues. In fact, this should be a complete record of the play, so that if the DSM is away for any reason, someone else can pick up the script and run the show. It is also used by the Stage Manager when taking an understudy rehearsal.

The Assistant Stage Manager or ASM

The ASM is often a jack of all trades. Specific tasks include the getting and making of props, the compiling of a props list, and once in performance the creation of a props table, and the responsibility of making sure that the actors have their personal props with them. The ASM has to help set up the room for rehearsal, to help mark out the set, to assist with difficult entrances and to strike and reset props in scene changes. An ASM may be asked to make tea and to help with costume changes and, most importantly, to sweep the stage.

THE FIRST PRODUCTION MEETING

At this meeting you will only need one person from each department. The Producer, if there is one, will have to be present, the Designer, the Carpenter, the Wardrobe Mistress, the Lighting and Sound person, the Stage Manager and of course yourself. The Designer will show his designs for the set and the

David Napman's model for a production of **Rookery Nook** *at* **GSA.**

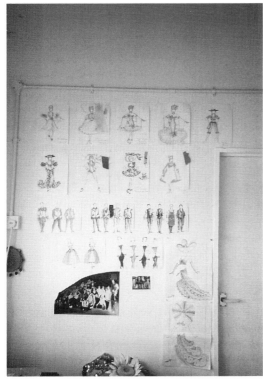

Costume designs pinned up on the wall of the wardrobe.

costumes. The Producer or Production Manager will give all the departments a rough idea about how much money is available to them in the budget. They will go away at the end of the meeting to work out how much they will have to spend. This could include special lighting effects and many changes of costume for all the cast. A date for a second meeting should be fixed before the meeting is closed.

THE SECOND PRODUCTION MEETING

All the departments will bring back their estimates and if all is well, the present design will be accepted. If this is not the case then certain adjustments have to be made to the design for the production to come within its budget. Once money is being spent on materials, receipts will need to be kept and accounts drawn up. A borrowing book needs to be organized for all the props that have been lent for the production. Deadlines have to be confirmed, and the transporting of scenery from workshop to theatre or school hall arranged. The actors' measurements including their shoe and hat sizes have to be taken and given to the Wardrobe Mistress, ideally before rehearsals start, so that he/she can get ahead with making the costumes, especially if it is a play with a large cast. The postal, e-mail addresses and phone numbers of all the cast and crew should be in the possession of stage management who can then contact everyone about the dates and times of rehearsals. You should now be ready to start rehearsals and begin another phase in the realization of your production.

In the following chapter, we will look at the choices a play can offer the designer. By this time you will have decided upon a concept for the play and with your designer will have made some drawings and plans of the proposed set and costumes. You will have a list of all the requirements for the play, which could range from a charabanc for a school trip (*Our Day Out*), to a thick fog (*The Dream*) or a desperate escape across a collapsing rope bridge (*Caucasian Chalk Circle*). It is these problems, together with the way in which the action of the play moves, that will have to be solved before you start rehearsals.

5 HOW THE PRODUCTION WILL LOOK

The designer needs to make as thorough a search of the play as the director. He will not only be visualizing how the play will appear to the audience, but creating an environment in which the action of the play can take place. The director has to encourage the designer not just to make pretty pictures, but allow one scene to follow easily after another so that the rhythm of the play and the dramatic action are continuous. Once the moving of large and clumsy pieces of scenery gets in the way of the action you are in trouble. You could find yourself, as the director, with the crucial decisions of having to ditch the set and performing the play on an empty stage. What a waste of money and time, not to mention the hours of hard labour the carpenter and painters had spent in making and painting it, and the huge artistic blow to the poor designer's morale.

Let us consider all the choices when thinking about design, from the smallest to the largest available space.

THE STUDIO AS A PERFORMANCE PLACE

Whatever size your studio is you will need to make a scale drawing of the floor plan showing the doors and windows and where all the electrical power points are. You will also need an elevation showing the height of the ceiling, the lighting grid if there is one and the height and width of all the entrances. If there is only one door then it has to be used by both audience and cast. If there is no facility for sophisticated lights then you need to address this problem. You have to decide if all the cast will sit and watch the whole performance either as a backing to the action or on the floor in front of the audience. Once the performance has started no late-comers can be admitted until a suitable place in the action occurs. Having analysed the play for location and scene structure you will have a good idea about how much space you will need. A 5-metre square for an acting area is a reasonable size to start with, but it is important for you to consider the size of your cast when making the final decision. If your studio is very small you will have to compromise.

PHYSICAL RELATIONSHIP BETWEEN ACTOR AND AUDIENCE

Working in flexible spaces can be very exciting as there are many choices for your design and the audience's relationship to the actors and the play.

End On is when the audience sits at one end of the room and the actors work at the other. This requires a back wall or cyclorama. The actors will need to enter the stage from either

The Open Stage

The open stage is when the audience and actors are in the same room. Some modern theatres are built without a proscenium arch. The Crucible Theatre in Sheffield, The Chichester Festival Theatre, the Stratford Ontario Festival Theatre and The Olivier Theatre in London are extreme examples and present the designer with different problems. The scenery is no longer flat but has to be three-dimensional and becomes more sculptural rather than pictorial.

The Crucible Theatre, Sheffield.

Health and Safety

Nowadays the authorities have very strict criteria regarding health and safety. In a formal theatre everything has to be fireproofed and a Fire Officer will inspect your set and costumes before the first performance to see that they fulfil the regulations. They will also look at entrances and exits to make sure that the audience can vacate the space in the event of an emergency. Some studios are built in the knowledge that they are going to be used for performance, and in remote places will carry a public performance licence. Please check with someone who knows about how many lamps you can use in the studio without damaging the system. You will need a power socket for the sound system.

side or from behind, or through the middle of the audience. If you have your actors entering from the back of the audience make sure that they can get there from the backstage area without disturbing the audience.

A *Thrust Stage* is when the acting area protrudes into the audience, placing your audience on three sides. This creates great intimacy but the director has to be aware of the sight lines, making sure that every member of the audience gets a good view. The back wall may need to be decorated but remember that some of the audience will only get a sideways view of it.

Avenue Arena is when the audience is seated on either side of the stage with spaces at either end for scenery exits and entrances. This shape is not suitable for all plays but works

61

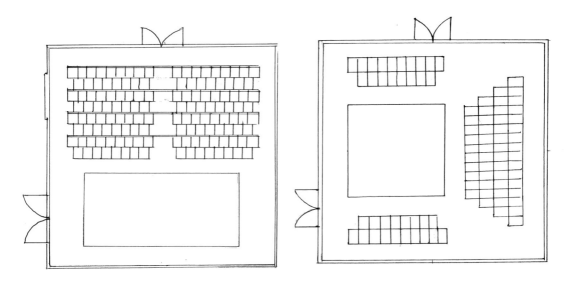

Studio plan for 'end on' format.

Studio plan for 'thrust' format.

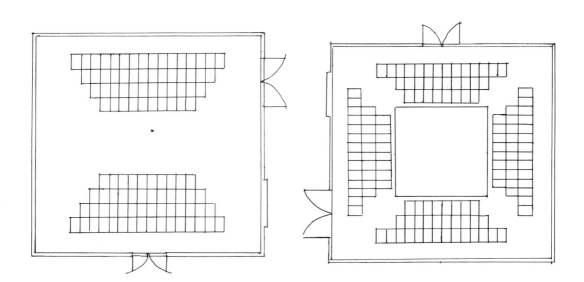

Studio plan for 'avenue' format.

Studio plan for 'in-the-round' format.

Sight Lines

These refer to the audience's view of the stage and the action. In a custom-built theatre the architect takes care of this so he either raises the acting area or he rakes the audience. Ideally in the above forms of seating the actor and the audience should start on the same level, so you may find that you will have to do the same with your audience. When deciding which form you will use, try out sight lines. In rehearsals, even dress rehearsals, there is no problem, but once the audience is seated, a gentle, intimate scene played on the floor it may not be visible to the majority of the audience and then it is too late.

well when the play demands some specific form of setting. It could work well with the *Caucasian Chalk Circle* or even *The Dream*.

In-the-Round is when the audience is seated all round the action. An example of this kind of theatre is the Stephen Joseph Theatre in Scarborough. Entrances are best made from opposite each other, or the performance area could be like the Circus Ring. A square with entrances in each corner is the most practical arrangement. The actors need to have access to all the entrances from the backstage area without being seen by the audience, and the director will have to find out how his actors are going to move in this space, and where the strongest positions are.

Promenade, another way of presenting a play, is when the whole space is empty of seats and the audience are free to move wherever the action takes place. The design can be very effective because the audience feels that they are right there, in the epic, and have become part of the world of the play. Keith Dewhurst's *Larkrise to Candleford* was written to be performed as a promenade. Simple scenery will add another dimension and stimulate the audience's imagination. The outside of a cottage can open to reveal a room inside, a hay cart can become the focus for a scene in a field, a bale of straw and we are in a barn.

The Mysteries by Tony Harrison were also written with this form of presentation in mind. Carts could be built, light and easy to move but big enough to accommodate whole scenes, and are not unlike those used by the guilds in

Promenade presentation of A Winter's Tale *(A&BC Theatre Company). Design by Colin Peters.*

Intimacy

When using in-the-round and three-sided arenas intimacy is essential, so the size of the audience is a priority. Once you get more than five rows deep there are problems. Not just the distance between actor and audience but seeing through other members of the audience. Also the warmth and proximity of the actor is lost. There are going to be times when you, as an audience member, will have an actor's back to you for some time. If you are near the actor he only needs to turn slightly for you to feel included.

A Truck

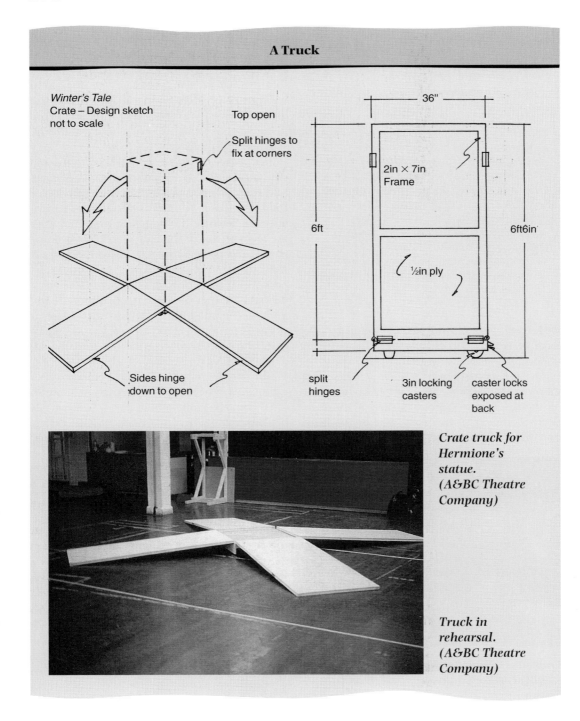

Winter's Tale
Crate – Design sketch
not to scale

Top open

Split hinges to
fix at corners

Sides hinge
down to open

split
hinges

36"

2in × 7in
Frame

6ft

½in ply

6ft6in

3in locking
casters

caster locks
exposed at
back

*Crate truck for
Hermione's
statue.
(A&BC Theatre
Company)*

*Truck in
rehearsal.
(A&BC Theatre
Company)*

A Truck *cont'd*

This is when a piece of scenery is built on wheels so that it can be pushed by two or even one person. The truck is just the base and the scenery can be built or attached onto it, even during the action. You might use it just for furniture, or it could be a many-sided structure representing different locations. In constructing it, get expert help and use smooth, well-oiled wheels that will swivel and can be locked when the truck is in position. Before deciding on using a truck make sure that the floor of your acting area is smooth and that there is enough room for it to manoeuvre, and that there is no rake.

Winter's Tale
Barrow – Design sketch
not to scale

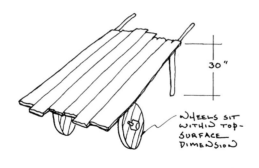

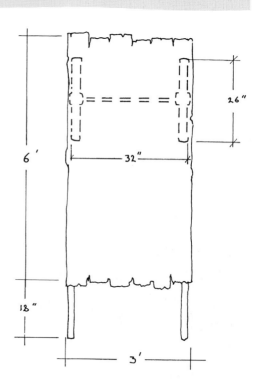

30 "

WHEELS SIT
WITHIN TOP-
SURFACE
DIMENSION

26 "

6 '

32 "

18 "

3 '

Design drawing of barrow, Colin Peters.

the streets when the plays were originally performed. It is important to make sure you do not sell too many tickets or attempt to use too big a space. The rehearsal period can be quite difficult because the actors find it hard to imagine the audience when it is not there, and though it appears to have an intimate atmosphere the actors still have to project, not only their voices but their characters as well.

The School Hall

The school play by tradition will have always been presented in the school hall on a 'letterbox-like' proscenium stage that is often awkward and inhospitable, but wonderful for accommodating the staff and Principal when the whole school is gathered for Assembly. It will often have a highly polished floor that is the pride of the caretaker. With care and tact it can become a far more flexible place than you originally thought. By adopting one of the above shapes you could find the stage an excellent place to accommodate some of your audience with the floor of the hall becoming your acting area. You might need to get your designer to make some more ground plans and elevation drawings of the hall, and its surroundings. This will help you to work out where the company will change, where scenery and furniture can be stored, and where the audience will go in the interval to have their cup of tea or glass of wine.

There may be problems as the hall is also used as a dining room and for PE, but if you are not overambitious and have a simple setting, you could assemble your staging in half an hour with the help of your actors and crew, and strike it at the end of the performance so that the hall is ready for Assembly in the morning.

Open Air Performances

There are often the most magical experiences both for audience and actor. To deliver a Shakespeare play into the ether gives the young actor a truly wonderful opportunity and a challenge in communication that no indoor theatre can provide. A leafy corner of your local park or the grassy banks of a river can offer you a natural setting that no designer could match. With a few carefully placed lights that can slowly take over from the dying rays of the summer sun, plays such as *As You Like It* or *The Dream* make perfect choices for alfresco performances. Of course you may need a few umbrellas ready or a pile of blankets to hand out to the less resilient members of the audience, but you will be providing them with not only material warmth but an unforgettable experience. However, there are a number of practical things to take into consideration.

Conventional use of hall.

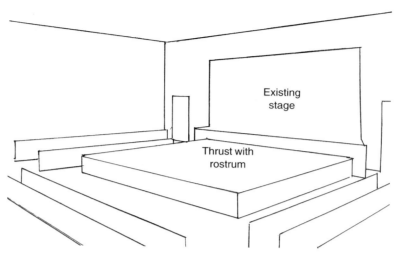

A thrust stage.

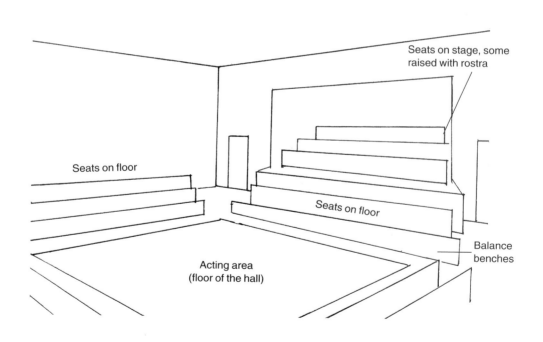

In-the-round.

* **The Design.** You could assume that, once you are out of doors, nature will look after your scenery, but a simple addition to a natural setting can provide an essential focus for the play. Some classical white benches for *The Dream* that can be covered with grass and flowery green drapes, once we move into the wood outside Athens, can become a place for Titania's Bower, somewhere for the lovers to fall asleep on, and once back in Theseus's Court a place for the lovers to watch the play-within-a-play of Pyramus and Thisbe.

* **Noise.** You have no control over aeroplanes but make sure you choose a site that is not near a major road or highway, and that there is an element of seclusion. If your audience are paying for the performance we have to consider their comfort, so their seating arrangements are important. Take care of the sight lines. Hire or borrow chairs that can be used out of doors. Ideally, the performance space should have some building or trees either behind or in front of them, for the actors' voices to bounce off. But remember if there is a wind, the rustling of leaves can be very distracting. I have experienced a play being performed in front of a country mansion with the audience facing the façade of the house, and also with the gardens providing the setting, with equal success.

The Tempest *in the rain, Sheffield Youth Theatre.*

* **Security.** The actors will need somewhere to change, to leave their clothes and valuables during the performance and to take refuge in if there is a storm. The dressing-room may not be near the performing space, so you need to ensure that they are secured before the performance starts. The same principle applies to leaving things overnight if you are doing more than one performance. Once it gets dark you will need security against vandalism as props and costumes discarded during the performance can easily go missing if they are left lying around and not collected up. So have a good supply of torches available.
* **Lavatories** need to be close by. If there are none, arrange for a few Portaloos to be placed in a nearby but secluded place for the audience and cast to use.
* **Power.** Make sure you have an electricity supply for your lights. There may be a handy supply point from the mains but if this is not possible you will have to hire a generator. Where you place the generator is important as they are noisy contraptions and can cause a distraction. However, they are a necessity and straw bales piled around the motor can deaden the sound.

It is a good idea to arrange one or two open-air performances before taking the company into a more formal space as it gives them a chance to open up and free their voices, minds and bodies. The joy of working with young actors is that you can go anywhere with them. Once you have gained their trust and given them confidence they will be brave and courageous because they carry very few preconceptions about the theatre with them.

Street Theatre

This follows many of the design disciplines you will find in Promenade but here visual impact and presentation is all important. There is an element of Mardi Gras and Festival about street theatre, for you are stopping the passer-by and hoping to engage them in your performance. You could be part of a street procession with large multi-operated puppets, tumblers, acrobats and fire-eaters as your characters. The essential elements are music songs, and telling the story visually rather than verbally. Your street theatre performance could be just a part of a larger event where your main performances are taking place in the ruins of a mediaeval castle, the local parish church, or down by the banks of the river.

Your Local Regional Theatre

There is nothing to make you nervous about presenting a production in a more conventional building, but a proscenium theatre is a formal place and your company of actors will have to become aware of how the space works. The design needs to be simple and effective. I started this chapter with a warning about filling the stage with scenery and I repeat that

Firth Park School dress-rehearsing a street theatre performance.

warning again. You have one big advantage over most professional companies in that you can present a play with really big casts.

To help make the floor of the stage into an interesting place the use of rostra can solve a lot of problems. They can divide the space up into different areas to become rooms in a house, or houses in a street. If the rostra are at different levels when the whole company has to enter – for example, to sing a song – everyone will be visible. A set comprising solely of rostra will serve plays like *Our Town*, *Under Milk Wood*, and *The Rimers of Eldritch*, and musical plays like *Oliver*.

Most theatre have a set of black drapes and if you ask for them to be hung not only as 'legs' but at the back of the set, they will mask off the backstage area and give you a neutral surround. They will offer you the choice of a black run of curtains at the back or the possibility of a white cyclorama. I would suggest you go for the cyclorama and ask for the back black curtains to be on a tab track which will mean you can open and close them from off-stage. This will offer two alternatives, either using the black background or, with the curtains open, the white cyclorama.

Good Lighting

This can make or break your production, and with a good lighting designer you can make the cyclorama a really magical area. With the use of coloured lamps and ground rows you can have a stormy sky or a glowing sunset. Clouds can be projected onto the backdrop and if you have enough money to hire a cloud machine they can move across the sky to represent the passing of time. It will be important to leave enough room between the back wall and the actors to avoid shadows.

Using the black background can be very effective as well. Here you will have to light the actors from either side. The lamps are hung behind the legs and if you have enough room about 3 metres above the stage level, which means that you will be lighting your actors from either side. This gives the actors a three dimensional look and takes the light off the black drapes. Just be careful when you are using a lot of black costumes that the actors do not disappear into the background.

Some very interesting lighting effects can be produced by using 'Gobos'. These are metal stencil-like slides that are used in lamps with lenses and become like a slide projection. You can make your own, buy them or hire them. They can make the stage floor look like the heart of a forest. You can make a projection of a church window or light coming into an attic.

When lighting a 'thrust' or 'in-the-round' setting care has to be taken to light the actors from more than one side, and you need to check all the areas of the auditorium to make sure lights are not shining in the audience's eyes, but more of this in Chapter 7.

Lighting and Sound Plots

There are two different kinds of lighting plots. One is how the lighting designer will want to place all his lamps either set around the stage or hung from the gird or as perches or ground rows. Your lighting designer will draw all these lamps on a ground plan. If your local theatre is helping you with the production, the professional in charge of the lights may do this. The other plot is a record of all the lighting states and changes that will take place during the play. A similar plot needs to be made in respect of sound effects. These plots may alter considerably during production week, so make sure an up-to-date version is kept, but there will be more about this in Chapter 7.

CONVENTIONAL SCENERY

You may decide that your play needs a more conventional approach or that your youth theatre has some scenery they have already used and may want to use again. *Flats* are constructed out of three-by-one timber and are like a large artist's canvas. The canvas is stretched across the frame and either nailed or stapled in place. It is then primed and fireproofed with a mixture of size, white paint and fireproofing. This stretches and gives a good base for painting the flats with whatever your stage designer has created. The flats are joined together by a cleat and line. The flats should be light, easy to handle and can be stacked against a wall. They are braced either by a French brace that is fixed to the flat by a hinge with a pin that can be removed, or an adaptable brace that is fixed to the flat by a large screw eye. These braces will have to be weighted so that the flats can stay upright. If they are well made you can create a very life-like room, and with enough backstage staff it can be struck and replaced with another set of flats in a relatively short time.

These are called *box sets* and are suitable for naturalistic plays. The flats can be made with holes in them to accommodate frames, either for single or double doors, windows, arches or fireplaces. Some carpenters who have worked in television use hardboard and commercial wallpaper, but the danger is that the flats can become heavy and cumbersome. To mask entrances and doorways you will need to make a backing or book flat which will need to be lit; this will give a sense of the world beyond the room in which the play or scene takes place.

When designing a play be careful how you mix conventions. You will need to decide upon a way of visually interpreting the play that suits it and also supports your interpretation as a director. Audiences are aware that they are watching a play and not a film, and they

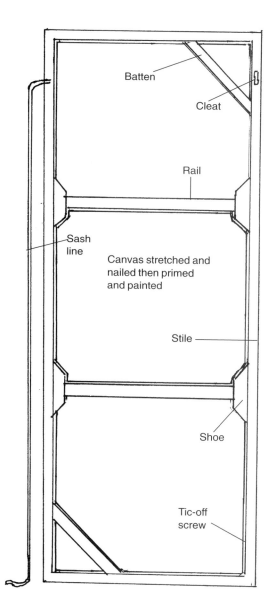

Drawing of a conventional flat.

are able to make allowances, and your young actors also have to understand the setting and interpretation so that they can feel it is also their way of seeing the play rather than accepting your design without understanding the thinking behind it.

THE COSTUMES

One of the many exciting things about being in a play is dressing up as someone else, and if you have a large cast the costumes can become a very expensive part of the budget. If you have an overall designer the look of the play should be taken care of, but be very careful about leaving the costumes to the individual actors. Their participation can be a great help but it has to be properly organized. The designer and wardrobe person need to get together to devise a basic costume. For example, a simple drawing of what is required can be circularized to every member of the cast, asking them to bring along, on a specific date, the articles of clothing and footwear required. Suggest that trousers, shirts and jackets can be purchased for very little at the local Oxfam or charity shop, so can old, white cotton sheets, bedspreads and blankets. With these basic materials and garments, along with some dyes from a local department store, you will be able to costume your play, and keep it within the budget. Again, creating the right convention or developing a house style for your company can mean the possibility of presenting a number of shows a year rather than one lavish one, as you will find that some costumes can be used again and again. Some youth theatres adopted a policy of dressing classical plays in modern dress. They may have strong aesthetic reasons for doing this, but it does help the young actor to behave in a natural way, allowing a freedom of physical expression.

Building up a stock of long skirts lined with bright primary colours can be invaluable and these can also double as cloaks. The same applies to black trousers that can be used by either sex, as can white or coloured shirts. Parents will be willing to hand on clothes their children have grown out of and a friendly and able parent can be a godsend working in the wardrobe as production week looms. Remember the costume only has to last the length of the run, but if you have invested more money in making 'good' costumes make sure you have them cleaned and stored after the production, and not taken home as a kind of trophy.

Hats, wigs and headdresses are part of the costume and care needs to be taken when selecting what, if any, the actor should wear. In dealing with a naturalistic setting, especially if it is in a specific period, research and accuracy are important but it is essential that we do not hide the actor beneath a load of unnecessary clothing. The actors need to look natural and at home in what they are given to wear, and should be encouraged to communicate to the audience the person they are representing in the story. Shoes should fit in with the costumes and if worn by a wealthy character should look clean and cared for, likewise a farmer's boots may need to have a touch of the farmyard about them. Check there is consistency about hair styles, length of hair and so on. Young people, especially boys, get very attached to their caps, and their removal and replacement can be quite a sensitive area, so this requires a firm but diplomatic approach.

PROPS

As we have seen in Chapter 4 the responsibility for the props comes under stage management, although some theatres have a property master. This job can be both fascinating and creative, and well-made and painted props can give a production a very classy look. Like the wardrobe department the work is interpretative, working from a picture or design given by the designer. In the youth theatre it can become a corporate activity that is not only great fun but gives the member a fresh investment into the production. The furniture is often part of the props department, as is china, tablecloths, swords and daggers, firearms, fans, umbrellas, canes, letters, books and so on. They are often divided into what is part of the setting and what is considered a personal prop.

MASKS

Let us start with the *Neutral mask* which is full and often white in colour and looks like the face of a mannequin model in a shop window. These can create a very sinister atmosphere. In some shops you will find these masks not only made out of white plastic but also in a clear plastic, which can create a dream-like effect. They can be uncomfortable to wear, but a little piece of sponge rubber placed strategically helps to alleviate the rubbing and scratching if they are not a good fit. It is also possible to make your own masks. All you need is a roll of brown gummed paper strips used for parcels, and papier mâché (newspaper and a flour and water paste). These home-made masks have a lot of character, but do not have the finished quality of the commercial plastic versions. The advantage is that they do fit the wearer who has created their own mask, and they have made it themselves.

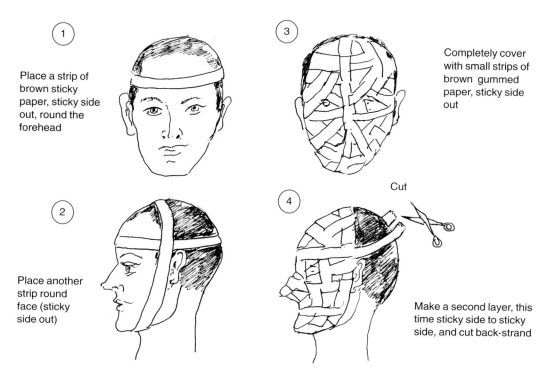

1 Place a strip of brown sticky paper, sticky side out, round the forehead

2 Place another strip round face (sticky side out)

3 Completely cover with small strips of brown gummed paper, sticky side out

Cut

4 Make a second layer, this time sticky side to sticky side, and cut back-strand

Making a mask from sticky brown paper strips.

Ready to apply papier mâché.

Applying papier mâché.

The finished product.

The Domino Mask

This is the small, usually black, mask that just covers the eyes and was very popular at masked balls in the sixteenth and seventeenth centuries. It is sometimes fixed by ribbon or elastic round the back of the head or held on a stick like a lorgnette, and can be highly decorated. In eighteenth-century Venice, masks were worn at social functions and owed something to the Commedia masks; they were often worn by both men and women with a Tricorn hat.

Traditional Masks

The Greek actors all wore masks that were big and elaborate, and many tribes in Africa, the Americas, and in the East have complex and beautifully designed masks that are used in their religious rituals and performances. Some of Brecht's plays suggest the use of masks, and

Commedia

The beautiful masks of the Italian *commedia dell'arte* can be purchased but are expensive. Each one is worn by a specific character, Arlecchino, Brighella, Pantalone and so on, and ideally should be used only in the context of the various *commedia* scenarios. Some are what are called half masks that allow the actor to use his own voice with subtlety. They can also be used by different actors to assume the same role. The *commedia* characters have a stylized way of speaking and moving.

there are many contemporary companies all over the world that specialize in the use of masks and create plays using only masked characters. It is an area of theatre that has

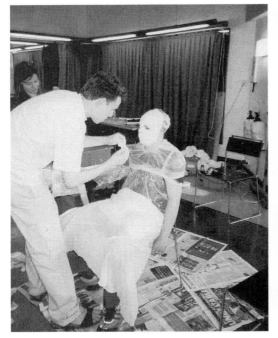

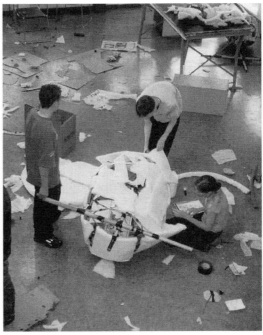

(Top) Russell Dean making a mask for a member of the Crucible Youth Theatre.

(Bottom) Gasmask-like monsters, Crucible Youth Theatre.

(Top Right) Russell and helpers creating a huge puppet for the Crucible Youth Theatre.

(Bottom Right) The finished puppet manned by three puppeteers.

enormous potential, and if entered into with intelligence and knowledge can suit a youth theatre company's work. Decide early on if you are going to use masks because the actors have to become accustomed to them and the way they influence the whole body.

MAKING YOUR OWN PROPS AND COSTUMES

If you are operating from within a school or college, a great deal of work can be carried out in various departments and made by the company members. It also allows the actors a chance to eventually rehearse in difficult or cumbersome costumes, rather than struggling with them at the last minute in a dress rehearsal. The more the actors have had a 'hands on' experience in the creation of the production, the more likely they are to look after their costumes and props, keep them in a good state of repair, and return them to a safe place once the rehearsals or fitting is over. The boys can learn to take up a hem, the girls to help build a rostrum and paint a flat. You should now be ready for the next stage of the production – the all-important rehearsal period.

6 THE REHEARSAL PERIOD

Let us start by looking at the rehearsal period with you, the all-important Director, and at what you need to bring to this period in the production's life. From the previous chapters we can see that a sound and practical knowledge of the play is essential, which will enable you to concentrate on watching your young actors at work, and be open to their moods and energies, rather than worrying about the play. Remember you have been living intimately with the text for some time whereas they are just being introduced to it. Your cast may come from the same school so they know each other, but it could be that your cast has been chosen from lots of different schools, some may be in further education or even earning their own living, so the group needs to form itself into a company of actors.

ESTABLISHING PATTERNS OF WORK

As I have stated earlier in this book, young people find the conventional way of rehearsing tedious. Each day has to work in its own right, so that the actors go away at the end of a rehearsal feeling a sense of progress, and are eager to have some rest, do whatever tasks they are set and arrive refreshed for the next day's work. Each day needs to be planned and divided up into activities. These activities have to complement each other so the

exercises, both technical and imaginative, that are carried out in the morning, can lead into more specific work on the text later in the day.

Your rehearsal period could be a few times a week over three to four months, or three weeks of concentrated rehearsal then straight into production. There are drawbacks and advantages in both methods of working. If there is more time then some of the following exercises can be explored in a leisurely fashion. It gives more time for the complex language and structure of a verse or classical play to settle, and for the actors to make the words and the characters their own. On the other hand, the pressure and excitement of a looming first night can spur the actors into action, and you will be amazed how much can be achieved in a short space of time.

ESSENTIALLY, THE REHEARSAL PERIOD SHOULD BE DIVIDED UP INTO THREE STAGES

Stage One
This is for preparation and exploration. Conventionally, on the first day of rehearsal there is a read-through. Some of your members might be very good actors but poor sight-readers, so to expose them and the company to such an ordeal is not beneficial. It is essential to lay down strong foundations, so establish some simple principles at the first

---

Example of Company Credo

Respect each other
Support of each idea
Compromise
Humour
Enjoyment
Willingness
Motivation
Communication
Focus
The whole is worth more than the sum of each
   part
Ensemble
Awareness of time
Dedication
Trust
Flexibility
Listening

Agreed qualities that make up a Company Credo.

meeting that could be called the *Company Credo*. This process should be done democratically, but with guidance. It should cover discipline, commitment, respect for each other and the work, and so on. These principles should be written down on a large piece of paper, making sure that everyone agrees. It forms a contract between everyone and should be displayed in a place for all to see throughout the rehearsal, the production period and all the performances.

Warm-Up Sessions

Tuning the body, mind and spirit for work should take place every day, but it should be chosen with discretion and be appropriate to the work planned for that day. The young actor may play an instrument – a violin, guitar or recorder, and they will appreciate the fact that to achieve success they need to feel at home with their instrument, to understand how it works and to be able to make it sing. They need to establish the same relationship with their own bodies and imaginations, and part of

your job is to help them towards achieving this. For instance, a long physical session followed by sitting still and working on text without physical action can be counter-productive, as the warmed muscles become stiff and cold. However, it will inform a session where the company is exploring the physical actions of a scene.

Always warm the voice up before a session that requires a lot of vocal passion and energy. On the other hand, a quick game of tag, stick in the mud, or basketball, can revitalize the company after a static period of discussion and cerebral work. As the director gets used to judging the mood of the company and what they need at any given moment, so the pattern of work will evolve organically.

The first stage of rehearsal should be over when you have explored the play at least once using some of the text strategies suggested or some of your own devising.

Learning Lines

During this period the company should not be expected to know their lines, but once parts are allocated, the actors should be encouraged to study and begin to memorize their parts. Excuses like 'But we haven't worked the scene yet' are not acceptable. All the exercises in this chapter are based on the play, and are there to help the actor understand it, and what they are saying and doing in the action. If they can't be bothered to learn their lines then there is always someone else to take their place. Some sound advice is: once a scene has been worked on in rehearsal, look at it that evening or next morning whilst things are still fresh in the mind and the body. Insist on accuracy and encourage others to help. Sitting with the text open on the lap, watching the television, is not the way to learn lines. It is best to sit at a table or move around the room, speaking the lines out into the ether. Every day, time should be set aside for study, learning and revision. Go over what was learnt the previous day, before tackling a new scene. Keep reading all the play and the lines that the other characters speak. Set a deadline for when all their lines should be learnt.

Character Work

Parallel to this, the early stages of character work should be taking place including any study out of rehearsal time, including the Stanislavsky lists (*see* p. 92) or any research needed for a further understanding of character and the specific environment of the play.

This period should also include exercise and strategies to help the actors understand the play – not only the words they have to say, but what they are doing with the words and how they affect the other characters in the scene. It is important to keep the company working together during the first stage, building the feeling of an ensemble, and involving everyone in the creative process.

Stage Two

This is the time in rehearsal when you start to look at specific scenes in more detail. Decisions need to be taken about how the actors are going to move and where they should be in the space in relation to the audience and their fellow actors. It should be a time for experiment, of listening and responding to the other characters in the scene, but to do this they need to be free of their texts, and secure in their words.

Divide the time up so that as a Director you can concentrate on individuals. Set aside a specific time for each scene and work out a rehearsal schedule that you will need to give to your Stage Manager and also put a copy on the notice-board for all to see.

Keeping Everyone Busy

Those not concerned in the scenes need to be allotted tasks, like hearing each other's lines, working on a scene on their own, or helping

Keeping everybody busy, Sheffield Youth Theatre.

with practical things like props and costumes. Keep everybody busy and remember if you have two casts they should attend all the rehearsals of their scenes. Idleness leads to boredom, and you get a disgruntled company. Changing work patterns is important as it brings new energies and disciplines into the work.

Sharing work

Once you have covered all the scenes in the play in this way you can start putting them together, but do not attempt to run the whole play until you feel confident that the cast have done enough work. Some scenes may be in better shape than others. This can depend on many issues, but it could be that some actors are being lazy about learning their text. Gathering the whole company together to see some of the work gives us all a chance to see how the work is progressing, and also gives the actors a chance to tell the story to more than just the Director.

Stage Three

There comes a time as Director when you have to hand the play over to the actors and let them find there own way through it. It is only then that they really experience what needs to be done. Our sense of nurturing and wanting them to be brilliant has to be put aside. If you have given them a healthy, detailed and inspiring preparation the play will begin to emerge. So the time has come for *the first run-through*.

This allows everyone to see it all fitting together. You will be able to see which scenes are working, and also where the work needs to be done. Those scenes that you have recently worked on may look better than earlier scenes. Some parts of the play may not have been worked on at all. After the run-through and a thorough note session, you will need to go through the play again, scene by scene. This is what I would call *tooth-combing the play*. This

---

The Big Scenes

Directors often like rehearsing the big scenes again and again. The trial in *The Merchant of Venice* for instance, or the closet scene in *Hamlet*, but remember it is the little scenes that help to make the big scenes work, so do not neglect them. If you get these scenes right the big ones will nearly always look after themselves.

---

can happen quickly and with energy and it lets the actors discover new things, to make sure those little moments that have never been explored are looked at in detail, and where the text keeps going awry. Let both casts have a go, and if you have time, swap casts around to give a freshness and new dynamic to the scenes.

The third stage of rehearsal should be completed with another run-through or two. Be wary of doing too many runs. There is plenty of time for that once the play is in performance. Always look at a scene or two before running the play again. Keep everyone on their toes. Make notes during a run or, if it is necessary, stop the rehearsal and solve the problem on the spot. That is the difference between rehearsing and performing.

The Note Session

After a run-through the cast are often tired and it is the end of the day, so be encouraging, and don't share any misgivings with them, but if they are being lazy let that be known. At the next day's rehearsal, write up your notes on large pieces of paper, and 'Blu-Tack' them to the floor for all to see and read. As people arrive let them read all the notes in a quiet atmosphere, and then sit quietly and go through the play, or a specific scene. Once everyone has read the notes, open up the discussion as to where the play is and what

Writing out notes for all to see, Sheffield Youth Theatre.

needs to be done. Once you have done the final runs in the rehearsal space you are now ready to go into production.

EXERCISES, GAMES AND STRATEGIES TO USE DURING THE DIFFERENT STAGES OF REHEARSAL

The Warm-Up

Listening

This is essential to all drama, so the listening circle described in Chapter 2 is a good way of starting the day. As people arrive in the rehearsal room, the basketball should be available, so that an impromptu game may start. Once you are ready to begin, form the circle and let everyone join one by one. Greet everyone with a handshake or an acknowledged look. With a large company that might

be the only direct contact you have with that person during that day.

Standing

If you have been in a circle listening it is an easy step to addressing standing still and in a well balanced manner. Everybody has a particular way of standing and walking. It is part of them and can tell us a lot about their personality. For the purposes of acting and becoming other people the actor needs to find a position of 'poised neutrality', which is the starting place for all their work. Little adjustments have to be made to the posture in order to produce this position. Maybe it is a tilt of the head or pelvis, or the weight is not evenly placed over the hips, the chin may be poking forward, or the shoulders tense. You may need to demonstrate on an actor the simple shifts that are needed to achieve this.

Physical Contact

The actors will often be in close and sometimes intimate contact with each other: lifting, embracing, fighting and carrying each other, so they need to get to grips with this early in rehearsal. You will find that at times you have to touch a member of the cast either moving them about the space or as suggested above to adjust their posture, but be careful. Ask the person you are about to touch if that is all right, and in such a voice that the whole room can hear, and explain why you are doing it. If you sense that they are uneasy with the idea ask for another volunteer. Young people are very aware of physical abuse and the last thing you want to face is being accused of this in one form or another. If in any doubt, get them to work on each other under your instruction.

Students rolling a partner across the floor. Photos: Alan Boyle

Let them form into pairs and adjust each other's posture without speech and with the passive partner closing their eyes so that they will sense where and how the pressure is being applied. This brings in an element of trust and focus, and the exercises in Chapter 2 can be used here if you think they are appropriate. They will also feel the difference in themselves where and how the adjustment is being made.

Sitting

Let each student have a chair and ask them to place it in the room so that they are spread evenly around, facing in different directions, and then ask them to sit. Ask them to look around the room just using their eyes and choose a person and observe the way they are sitting. Then, on a given instruction let them assume that way of sitting. Using their eyes again let them see and sense how the room has altered and what it feels like to be sitting like somebody else. Let this be done in silence and afterwards let them share their observations. To finish this part of the exercise let them assume a position of 'poised neutrality'. Feet should be flat on the floor, legs uncrossed, backs straight, arms and hands relaxed, eyes open and alive. You can repeat this again starting from neutral and transforming from themselves to someone else in the room and back again. This exercise is a simple way of finding out how to become somebody else and what it feels like. Changing the outside affects how you feel inside. Later in this chapter, we will see how we can adapt this exercise into a simple and effective way of becoming a character.

Lying Down

Instruct them now to lie on the floor in the semi-supine position described in Chapter 2. Their hands should be palm downwards and resting on that little triangle where the ribs end and the stomach begins. This position is an excellent one for proceeding with breathing and then into using their voices, for a further investigation into their anatomy, or into the awareness of tension and relaxation. Let the actor feel the rise and fall of the diaphragm and also become aware of his heartbeat. Let the heartbeat and the breathing settle into a natural rhythm. This is very calming and gives a good focus for those newcomers who are feeling anxious and nervous.

Tension and Relaxation

We are now going to look at tensing particular parts of the body. Start with the feet or the hands clenching and releasing the fists, and in this way work through the body paying particular attention to jaws, chest and buttocks, calves and thighs. The next stage is to instruct them to tense the whole body but continue to breathe, encouraging them to keep the throat free. Then to sense how they feel once the tension is released.

Walking

In the early stages of rehearsal it is important for the actors to practise moving about the space in an ordered fashion. First let them walk round the perimeter of the room leaving space between each actor and finding a common pace and way of walking. Observe how other people walk. Now let them fill the space with movement. They can follow someone and imitate their walk. They can run in the space and pass each other with a look or gentle touch saying 'hello'. They can stop suddenly, move backwards and sideways. They can move as if they are thistledown or as heavy clay. Work with a drumbeat or tambourine, getting them to obey the instrument.

Crossing the diagonal of the room in pairs to a slow drumbeat or slow processional music can follow this. Each pair must find the right moment to enter the space to keep a

continuous flow of energy and movement. This is also good practice for timing. The manner in which they walk should be as neutral as possible. The balance should always be good and the feet working from sole to heel. The backs should be straight and the head and shoulders free from tension. Suggest they add imagination to the exercise, and changes of pace and rhythm, so they could be soldiers returning from a battle, brothers and sisters at the funeral of their father, officials at a coronation, even tired mechanicals returning from a rehearsal in the wood outside Athens.

Using the Diagonals with Music

Having discovered the diagonal let them use the perimeter and the diagonal following them as if they were paths in a formal garden or town square. They can move in any direction but must always stick to the imaginary paths. Start the exercise with everyone standing around the perimeter, and give them some music to move to (perhaps the Purcell suggested in Chapter 2). The music has to start before they can move. The formality of the music and the designated paths control where

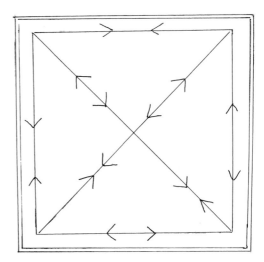

Travelling exercise showing pathways.

Static and Dynamic Tension

In order to perform, the body needs to be aware of some form of tension. To become a character in a specific emotional and psychological state, the actor has to be aware of how the energy in his or her body is being used. The very talented actor has a natural technique and instinctively uses static and dynamic tension with both body and mind, but not always consciously. The less talented can learn, but under pressure and in order to please either their director or themselves he or she will often try too hard. This is when damage can occur and lack of clarity can mar a good performance. He/she has to be in control of the body, yet still allow the imagination to inform the action that lies at the heart of an actor's technique. Dynamic tension is like the words of the text, static tension is like the punctuation.

they are able go. Let them feel free to express themselves within these disciplines. Observe how they respond to the exercise and let the music play through to the end. Share observations and let them have another go. Allow them to build relationships, have arguments, build scenarios, but without the use of speech; let their bodies do the talking.

This exercise gives the actor an awareness of the space in which they are working and the other actors in it. An awareness of their internal space is essential together with the ability to control it.

THE VOICE

A warm body and an awareness of everyone else in the space helps to prepare the young actor for the day's work. Once the body is warm it is easier to do some specific work on the voice. To separate the two in acting is nigh on impossible as they work together in expressing and communicating the story and, although they can be looked at separately, should always be considered as one.

Warming up the Voice

To start working on the voice let the actors lie on the floor, and if the previous session has been very active suggest that they have a sweater handy so that they don't get cold. Place the hands on the diaphragm and get them to breathe. If their pulse is racing let the breath and heartbeat settle. Once that has happened, suggest a gentle hum. Let them take a breath whenever they need to, but the hum must not stop. They have to take responsibility for its continuance. They should have a tingling buzz on their lips. They must listen to their own sound as well as all the other voices in the room.

Once there is a good hum going the next step is to create an *Ah sound* (as in arm). The tongue should be relaxed with the tip behind the teeth. Let the open sound grow out of the hum so that on a given instruction their lips open with a relaxed jaw and they let a nice clear sound come out. (This sound gives a clear indication about the state of the company. Sometimes it is a horrid discordant noise, sometimes it is quite beautiful. Do not communicate this observation to the group, but note it for yourself.) Suggest that they play with the sound, high and low, loud and soft, but the overall sound of the group must not die away. This is important because at this stage the actor wants to be free to express him/herself without judgement. Move amongst the actors as they work, listen and observe how they are responding to the exercise. Turn the hum into an *Ooh sound* (glue), an open mouth just bringing the lips into a circle to make the sound, and then into an *Eeh sound* (sea), an open mouth, lifting the back of the tongue. Let them play with the three sounds, going from one to the other. If this is their first session you have probably done enough. So complete the exercise by falling silent and then get them all to turn on to their right sides. Suggest they visualize how they will slowly get to their feet. If they get up too quickly they could feel light-headed or even pass out, so do it slowly. A good idea is to bring them to a sitting position, and then have a shared conversation about what they have experienced and heard. Once the group is used to doing the vocal warm-up, there is no need to always start it on the floor. Acting is about moving and speaking, so there is no reason why you cannot do a combined physical and verbal warm-up, but make sure you know what the priorities are.

Tongue-Twisters

Teach them a simple tongue-twister. Here are a few difficult ones:

'Popocatepetl, copper-plated kettle, plate of bread and butter, red and yellow leather'; 'She sat upon the balcony inexplicably mimicking him hiccuping, and amicably welcoming him in.'

Initially their success rate will be poor, so the actors' lack of success leads very conveniently into asking them what needs to be done to achieve success. It becomes easier if the actor takes his time; also familiarity with the words means you can focus on what the lips, tongue and teeth are doing, rather than trying to remember the words, but most important of all, muscles that have never been used before need to be awakened and exercised.

Articulation Exercises

The Tongue

Start by sticking the tongue out, making it fat, making it flat, curling the tip up to touch the nose and curling it down to touch the chin.

These exercises can be great fun and cause a lot of mirth.

The Facial Muscles

Chewing an imaginary crunchy apple gets the face muscles and the jaw working. Start this by making a long face, a wide face, and a tiny face and slowly lead them into chewing the apple.

The Lips, Tongue and Teeth

Sounding all the consonants in the alphabet leaving out the vowels, as follows:

'Bippity boppity boo, Cippity coppity coo, Dippity, doppity doo', and so on through to the end of the alphabet.

The Breath

Seeing how far they can count on a single breath. Once they have become accustomed to the exercises, let them proceed with the tongue-twisters.

Singing Rounds

Singing goes down well; start with a simple round like 'London's Burning'. If you cannot keep a tune, get someone in the company to teach it to the others. Do this by rote, a phrase at a time, so they learn through the listening.

Once they've learnt it, divide them up into four groups and sing the round. Then get them to move around the room, singing to each other and eventually returning to their group.

Everyone Can Sing

Some people are very nervous about singing, and will have been told they will never sing, because they cannot hold a tune. This is not true. Assume that everyone can sing like angels, and they will.

Another favourite is the 'Grand Old Duke of York'. You sing it through four times at a good pace. The first time sing the verse through straight, then leave out the word 'up', leave out the word 'down', and lastly leave out the words 'up' and 'down'.

'The Grand Old Duke of York'
He had ten thousand men.
He marched them up to the top of the hill,
And he marched them down again,
And when they were up, they were up,
And when they were down, they were down,
And when they were only half-way up
They were neither up nor down.

MUSICALS

Learning Songs
If the play contains a lot of songs or you have chosen a full-scale musical, you will have to schedule plenty of time for the company to have a singing warm-up. This should include scales, tuning and tone. The technique involved in singing is almost identical to that for the speaking voice, but like all teaching methods there are variations, and you will need to take these into consideration. Start to teach the music early on in the rehearsal, combining tune and lyric all the time, and again leave plenty of time for this. The actor/singers have to know the lyrics, tune and harmonies very well before they start to move about in the space. If they are familiar with the music and how it sounds they will be able to make the necessary adjustments.

Choreography
This also has to be taught or devised and then set by the choreographer, or movement director. Motifs and steps can be added to the physical warm-up, so that the company will begin to learn the physical language of the piece in a gentle and less stressful atmosphere.

Again assume that everyone can dance.

The work on the voice is not for them to try and speak 'proper' but to improve their ability to communicate vocally, to find notes and colours in their voices so that they can bring the words, emotions and ideas in the play alive, and that they can fill a large space with a clear unforced sound They will need to learn some text to use in these sessions. Let them choose a piece themselves, something from the play, but not necessarily from the character they are going to be.

WORKING WITH THE TEXT

Until the actors have learnt their lines it is difficult to find ways of exploring the play practically. Some directors will have worked out all the movements of the characters before the rehearsal starts and will spend the first rehearsals telling everybody where they have to go. This is called blocking the play and if there are lots of people in the scene it is a way of solving the problems of entrances, sight lines and exits. At times, it is necessary to support the company in this way. It is however a tedious process and one that can become very boring, if every line of the play is explored in this way. There are other ways of working.

Casting

It is a good idea not to have understudies but to have two casts so that everyone is fully occupied. If you have a big part in one cast you have a small one in the other cast. This helps during rehearsals if, for one reason or another, a member of the company is away. It also helps to create a generous company attitude, together with an element of healthy competition.

Getting to Know the Text

It should be the responsibility of the whole cast to know the play well. They should be encouraged to read it in their own time, but do not assume that they have done this, and remember your own personal struggle in coming to terms with the text and its meaning. Commencing work on the play doesn't necessarily mean you have to start with the first scene. Choose a moment in the play where there is plenty of action. Let us take for example two scenes from *A Midsummer Night's Dream,* Act Two Scene One and Two. You will have previously divided the scenes into units. The two scenes divide up into six main units. Unit 1: Puck and Fairy. Unit 2: Oberon, Titania and Puck. Unit 3: Demetrius and Helena. Unit 4: Oberon and Puck. Unit 5: Titania, Oberon and Fairies. Unit 6: Lysander, Hermia, Puck, Helena and Demetrius. You are going to ask the company to create some tableaux showing the dramatic development of their particular unit using only the information contained in their section of the text.

Workable Copies of the Text

For the purpose of the exercise, photocopy the scenes with any cuts you might have made, with enough copies so that everyone has a script to work with. There are about twenty parts available in the units, so work out how many scenes you need in order to give everyone something to do. Divide the company into groups of two, three and five to accommodate the number of characters in each of the units, and it doesn't matter if more than one group work on the same unit.

Instruct them to read aloud to each other, only coping with as much text as they feel happy with. They will find this quite difficult, but it is good practice. Set a given time for the task and circulate amongst the groups to find out how they are progressing and which ones are the good sight-readers. Without getting involved in a group discussion help to answer questions and see whether they have sufficient information to move onto the next stage.

Get them to write down words that puzzle them, and have a good dictionary or a thesaurus at hand. Let them discover what is happening in their section, where it is

Working on the text in small groups with Meg Jepson.

happening, who the characters are, and the dramatic highlights. Now let them work on their tableaux, again not allowing them too much time, so as to give a sense of urgency to the exercise. They will be working instinctively and with a certain amount of competition because they know that they will have to show their work to the rest of the group. Encourage them to be precise and to back up their decisions with words or phrases from the play.

Sharing the Work

Once they have worked something out don't let them over-rehearse. The exercise is then shared in the same way as was done with the four seasons exercise in Chapter 2. You could support it with music or the company might want to create a magic soundscape of humming and singing. The main purpose is for them to experience and witness the dramatic development of the play, to find out who the characters are, to arouse their curiosity as to what will happen next, to get a taste of the language, and have a sense of responsibility for the development of their work.

Once we have seen the tableaux melting one into another we will get a feeling for the play and its changing moods, something of Oberon's character and that of mischievous Puck, poor Helena and vulnerable Hermia. It is very valuable to revisit the tableaux a second time and we can do this in a similar way to the clay statues exercise in Chapter 2.

Of course this is only a beginning but the actors are already physically entering into the world of the play and getting a taste of the characters, and what will be required of them as performers. They experience the energy and integrity required to sustain the tableau over a period of time, and the concept of static and dynamic tension mentioned earlier in this chapter. The whole play can be explored in this way and the story clarified. Once this process is completed a good way to finish is for the company to divide into small groups of four or five actors and to create 'The Trailer' of the play. Let them use storytelling techniques, sound effects and voice-overs. Let them share their trailers in a 'showing' and enjoy seeing each other perform.

Removing Punctuation

When working on a play in verse with long sentences the following exercise not only improves the listening, but also clarifies the language. When we are sight-reading we automatically obey the punctuation; it helps us to unravel the sense, to give us space to breathe, and to hear what the character is saying. Take a speech of a character of some ten to fifteen lines of iambic pentameter and remove (using the computer) all the punctuation and the line endings. The following is from a speech by Titania, complete with punctuation.

Come now, a roundel and a fairy song;
Then, for the third part of a minute, hence:
Some to kill cankers in the musk-rose buds;
Some war with rere-mice for their leathern wings,
To make my small elves coats; and some keep back
The clamorous owl that nightly hoots and wonders
At our quaint spirits. Sing me now asleep;
Then to your offices, and let me rest.

This will now become:

come now a roundel and a fairy song then for the third part of a minute hence some to kill cankers in the musk rose buds some war with rere mice for their leathern wings to make my small elves coats and some keep back the clamorous owl that nightly hoots and wonders at our quaint spirits sing me now asleep then to your offices and let me rest.

89

"Philomel with melody sing in our sweet lullaby"

"Churl, upon thy eyes throw all the power this charm both owe."

"Nay, Good Lysander; for my sake, My Dear, lie further off yet; do not lie so near."

"And sometimes lurk in a gossip's bowl"

"Ill met by moonlight proud Titania"

"Yet marked I where the bolt of cupid fell"

"You draw me, you hard-hearted adament"

Drawings of tableaux with quotes from the play.

The company sit making a circle. Everyone has a copy of the unpunctuated speech lying face downwards before them. A volunteer starts by lifting the paper and immediately reading aloud, with no pause to try and look ahead or make some sense of it before uttering. The volunteer continues until he or she is challenged by someone in the circle. All they need to do is knock once on the floor, if they haven't understood what is being said. The reader puts the paper face downwards on the floor and the challenger picks up his text and starts reading aloud from the begining of the speech. Another challenge is made, or the reader loses track and gives up. Through the listening and the words alone the sense of the speech is slowly unravelled.

This exercise takes quite a long time, and everybody should have a go, but it is not a good idea to do this exercise with a company of actors who have problems with reading.

Feeding the Text to Each Other

Another way of exploring the play is to have two people being made responsible for each character. This works very well if you have two casts. One of the actors holds the text and feeds the other actor the lines. They keep close by their other half without getting in the way of the action and clearly but quietly feed a phrase or short sentence to the speaker. The speaker can then deliver his lines to the other characters in the scene, speaking directly to them, free to interpret them as he chooses. He is also free to move about wherever he wants, to touch the other actors, to look them in the eye, and to listen to what is being said without having constantly to refer to his text.

Text, Improvised Text, Text Again

A simple text strategy is to take a scene from the play and let the actors go through it reading from the text, but trying out how and where they will move. The script is then put aside and the actors improvise their way through the scene using their own words to express what their characters are doing and saying to each other. They should be encouraged to use their own words, but try to achieve their objectives, their character's wants and needs. The improvisation is then discussed and the actors pick up their scripts and go through the scene a third time using the words given them by the playwright but now using the experience of the improvisation as well. This will often move the scene on, and offer the actor another set of choices. It also reveals whether the actor knows what his character really wants from the scene. However, with this exercise they should have a good knowledge of the scene before they start, and have given it some thought. Therefore, if you plan to try this exercise let the actors know the day before so that they can do their homework.

Physically Exploring the Scenes

Once you feel the actors are becoming familiar with the scenes and their function in the dramatic development of the plot, once they are begin to sense how their character will move and behave, they are now ready to give some shape to the scenes they are in, to make some decision about how the scene will go and where the climaxes will happen.

BEGINNING TO WORK WITHOUT THE BOOK

It is now time for them to work on the scenes in detail. This can be done by dividing the company into scene groups, allowing them to work with the other actors in the scene, with a company member not directly involved watching the scene and reporting back what is seen and heard. This person is fulfilling the role of the director, which means that you can have a number of different scenes happening at one time, and you are free to go from group to group to see how they are progressing. If all is going well do not interfere, and let them solve the problems of the scene. If they are wandering away from the truth of the scene or are arguing unnecessarily, become a mediator or even take over from the student director for a while. They should now be working without a script though it might be necessary for them to have it by them for reference. Once they become confident and begin to enjoy rehearsing, the text can take a less important role in the scene. A check on accuracy, not only of the words but also the punctuation, needs to be kept. This process is very important and every scene in the play needs to be explored in this way. At the end of a good rehearsal, share the work even if it is only a few lines, so that the actors know where their work stands compared with the others.

WORKING ON CHARACTER

Acting gives the individual the opportunity to become somebody else. A good playwright has, either through instinct or craft, created a rounded flesh and blood person. They have a past and present, they have both good qualities and bad qualities and a complex and interesting psychology. They are placed in situations that challenge their integrity and test their morality. Creating the great characters like Hamlet or Hedda Gabler, Mother Courage or Beatty Bryant can prove quite a daunting task for the actor to realize, but they can also be a gift to the right actor, who naturally transforms himself, submits to the character and allows it to enter into his body, mind and soul. We need to look at what we can do to help those people who are not blessed with extraordinary talent.

If our play has a market scene or a crowd of people and we want to fill the stage with action and real people, doing the above exercise can bring genuine life to the scene.

THE STANISLAVSKY LISTS

It is a good habit for the actor to keep a notebook during rehearsals. This not only keeps track of what has happened day to day, but there are tasks to be done on the text in connection with their character. One of these tasks is to make a series of lists. Earlier in the book I suggested the lists that the director needs to make from the play to help with the design and interpretation of the play; similarly, the actor can make his own personal character search.

The first list is what the character says about himself. Write down the exact words he says. Little things like, 'I am sorry', 'I don't know about that', 'In my opinion . . .' tell us a great deal. There are also bigger, more dramatic things like Juliet's 'Romeo, Romeo, wherefore art thou Romeo, deny thy father and refuse thy name and I'll no longer be a Capulet.' These few lines tell us not only about Juliet but also about Romeo, which leads me onto the second list. This is what the character says about other people in the play.

The third list is what other people in the play say about your character. These lists can be shared, or referred to when unsure about the development of your character, but in making them we begin to read the text from a very specific angle. A list of what the character does in the play is also valuable. We then discover how much is fact and how much we need to make up to create a rounded character. In a good naturalistic play many of these facts have been taken care of by the playwright, but in a more obscure text these exercises force us to look at everything in the play and not just our own part.

OBSERVATION

A good exercise for the early days of rehearsal is to let the actors observe humanity. Let them choose a partner. Together they are going to go out into the town and observe people going about their personal business. They should eavesdrop on conversations; see how an elderly person crosses the road; watch someone buying a hat for a wedding, or a cardigan for an unwilling husband; watch meetings of relatives at a station; someone hiring a taxi or getting on a bus.

They then bring back these characters to the rehearsal space and, either as a still picture or an enactment of what they have heard and seen, share it with the rest of the company. There is an element of mimicry in this exercise, of taking what we observe of the outside, but the effort needed by a crippled, elderly person to walk, or the ease with which a child skips ahead of its mother both have an emotional quality that take them out of the ordinary and the actor has to internalize that effort.

IMAGING

This is an extension of the sitting exercise explained earlier in this chapter. The company sit, with eyes closed and you ask them to clear 'the screen' in front of them. They are now going to think about their character or a character in the play that interests them. On their imaginary screen they are now going to build that character. Suggest that they start with an outline, a silhouette of the character and then, like scraping off the number on a lottery card or doing a brass-rubbing, they begin to reveal the character. Suggest that they can start with the hands, and then the body, see where they are, in a room or outside. What are they wearing? What are they doing?

Once you have fed them enough suggestions go round each person, lightly

Observing at the market.

A busker.

Taking the shopping home.

touching them on the shoulder, and ask them to tell us what they see in their picture, all this with the eyes still closed. Go round everyone in the room staggering them so that the voice will come from all around. If they are speaking too softly encourage them to speak up.

When everyone has had their turn, ask them to now become the person in the picture. Suggest that once they have assumed the position they get up from the chair and move around the room. Once moving they can add a line of dialogue that they can repeat to themselves or to someone else. Encourage them to try the different moods of the character, to explore moments of stillness and activity.

THE ANIMAL IN YOUR CHARACTER

A liberating and exciting exercise to try when working on character is to become the animal in your character. We all have our own animal, the one we like best or the one someone else might choose for us. The character that the actor is exploring might have the characteristics of some animal, for example Cleopatra could be like a cat, Helena in the *Dream* like a giraffe.

The actor chooses what they think is an appropriate animal and does some research, about its habitat, what food it eats, how and where it raises its young; it could be a shark, or a robin, or a domestic cat. Start the session with a circle and the company speaking about their choice of animal. Once we have heard about everyone's choice of animal, let them find a place on the floor and curl up. Again like the imaging exercise, let them slowly transform into the animal. Let them choose where they are and what they are doing. Suggest they try lots of different activities. Also remind them that animals have no psychology, their appetites are immediate, they are hungry, they are tired, they are sexy, and they are frightened. Allow them to play with their animal and with each other. Let them try out their animal noises.

It may take more than one session for them to feel completely at home, however it is important for them to apply it to the play in hand. They need to have a piece of text available, something that they have learnt and feel at home with. They then have to try and transform into the animal whilst speaking the text as the character. They find out how the animal affects the character's speech and

Animals confronting each other. Photo: Alan Boyle

Students creating relationships between pet and master. 'There's a good dog'. Photo: Alan Boyle

'Come here boy!' Photo: Alan Boyle

movement. They can then transform back again. This exercise will release emotions and feelings in the actor that have remained dormant. It can also unearth extremes of character that help when playing comedy; and mannerisms and physical motifs, other then their own, that they can begin to use in rehearsal.

PUTTING CHARACTERS TO THE TEST

Sometime during the second stage of the rehearsal period, the following exercise is very useful as it allows the actors to wholly inhabit their characters without having to worry about knowing too much text. They choose three contrasting phrases or sentences used by

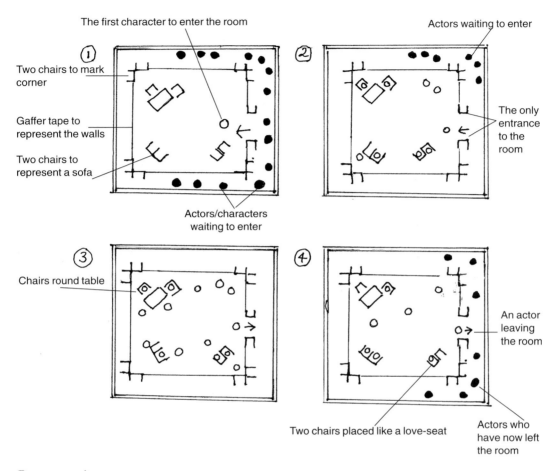

The first character to enter the room

Two chairs to mark corner

Gaffer tape to represent the walls

Two chairs to represent a sofa

Actors/characters waiting to enter

Actors waiting to enter

The only entrance to the room

Chairs round table

An actor leaving the room

Two chairs placed like a love-seat

Actors who have now left the room

Room exercise.

their character, and make sure they are secure in the words.

Arrange the room with chairs in such a way that it represents a room in a house. Mark out where the entrance to the room is and place some furniture around the space, representing sofas, desks and chairs. The actors, in character, enter the room one at a time. They can move anywhere, sit and stand but communicate verbally only with their chosen phrases. Nobody can leave the room until everyone has entered. Only then can people

make an exit. Encourage them to communicate with each other, but try not to all speak at once. They should be aware of everyone's presence, and should react accordingly, especially when a new character enters the space, or when someone leaves it. The exercise starts and finishes with an empty room.

This allows the director to observe how the characters are developing, and some people will be freed by this exercise, where previous worries about remembering the text are removed.

CONCLUDING THE DAY OR THE WHOLE OF THE REHEARSAL PERIOD

Not all the above exercises will be suitable for your production, so it is up to your discretion as to how you use them. Make a note of the ones that get a good response, as well as those exercises that don't appear to work. Disturbance in the company can often occur when they are struggling for understanding. If the day ends badly or there has been some feeling of unrest, complete the session without making any judgemental comments. Starting the next day you could question how the day before went, and the problems will surface easily. If the day's work has gone well let it be publicly acknowledged – we all need encouragement. It may be necessary for people to make observations that are not always complimentary, but they have to find a way of making constructive criticism that is neither too personal nor cruel.

If you can work organically and sense when the time has come to enter the third stage of rehearsal, the actors will really enjoy joining all the scenes together, and you will have a chance to see what needs to happen next. It also gives the technical team an opportunity to see how the play is developing, and to question some of the things that are happening from their perspective – for example, the scene and costume changes and the lighting and sound cues.

7   STAGE COMBAT

A play will often contain some form of physical combat, either between two individuals (Hamlet and Laertes) or a massed fight (the opening of *Romeo and Juliet*). If these physical conflicts require sword play of any kind you will need the help of a trained and experienced swordsman to teach and set the fights for you, and actors who are able to pick up the rudiments of fencing without too much difficulty. However, a well organized and executed stage fight adds excitement to a production and can be an enormously enjoyable experience for the participants, and well within your capabilities if approached with care.

Before letting the young actors loose on the scene through improvisation they will need to have certain basic skills at their fingertips. These can be introduced through a series of games and exercises, which could become part of your routine physical warm-up. Many of the exercises I have described in this and other chapters concern the participants having a confident approach to physical contact with each other. The more they do 'weight taking' and are happy with going to the floor and having a speedy recovery to the upright position, the better. So an awareness of the space and the people in it, and a readiness to stop and then start movement on a drum beat are essential.

THE TWO MAN WARM-UP

This is an excellent warm-up for the beginning of any physical work that requires contact and the use of the back, and sensitivity to your partner's rhythm and needs. The company works in pairs. One of the two gives the warm-up, the other receives it. Once completed, the roles are reversed. It is not a 'touchy feely' exercise, but concerns the giving and receiving of energy and an awareness of breath on both parties.

Stage One
Actor A stands and waits to receive the warm-up. Actor B, just using his hands, no words, places his hand on A's back and pushes him gently but firmly over, so that A is hanging from the waist, knees slightly bent, head and shoulders loose. B massages the lower back with brisk and fast movement, warming up the base of the spine and the lower back. With fast, light but firm movements, he warms up the arms and hands and legs with the flat of the hand; he then returns to the back and with gentle but firm movements pushes the torso from side to side and up and down, swinging it so that the arms and head are loose and floppy.

Stage Two – the Side Stretch
With Actor A still hanging from the waist, B now stands to one side of A and places one

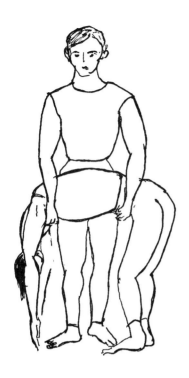

Position side for stretch on exhalation of breath. . .

So he can fall onto his partner's back.

hand under A's armpit and the other on the top of the pelvis, getting a secure hand-hold, with A giving B his weight. The pair coincide their breathing, and on an outgoing breath B lifts and stretches A's side against his stomach, then gently releases A. He then goes to other side and repeats the stretch on the other side.

Stage Three – the Back Stretch

B, now standing behind A, bends down and places his shoulder against A's backside, keeping his back straight to form a flat surface for A to fall back on. He then places his hands on A's lower ribs so that he can feel A's breathing, and on an outgoing breath he flicks A's torso up so that he can fall back on to B's back (as in weight taking). B flicks the base of his spine as a signal for A to return to an upright position.

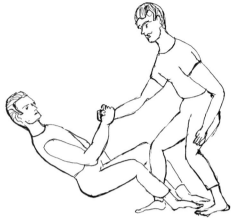

Dropping down, supported by partner.

Getting up on impulse from partner, pelvis first.

Stage Four – Reactions

A lifts B's arms to the side (crucifix), and with delicate cutting movements and using both hands cuts the wrist, indicating for A to release wrists. This is also done with elbows and armpits. B can flick the arms back into position whenever he wishes, so that he can observe how quickly and accurately his partner reacts.

The process is repeated after changing partners. Once both partners are warmed-up, and only until then, Stage Five is added.

Stage Five

This comprises dropping to the floor and getting up again on a given impulse. The partners stand opposite each other, holding their right hands at chest level. A gentle tap on the shoulder from one partner is the impulse for the other partner to drop to the floor, using the other partner's hand for support while dropping down through bents legs and the spine. The supporting partner must make sure that his feet are on either side of one of his partner's. Once flat on the floor, the hands still joined, the supporting partner gives a flicking

impulse with his hand and the prostrate one uses this impulse to rise to his feet, leading with his pelvis. With practice this can become an enjoyable and invigorating exercise, but the back must be warmed up first.

SOME SIMPLE GAMES AND EXERCISES

Grandmother's Footsteps

Grandmother stands at one end of the room with her back to the rest of the company, who line up at the other end of the room. The purpose of the game is for someone to touch Grandmother without being spotted moving. Grandmother keeps her back to the group but can turn at any time to catch individuals out. If you are caught moving you return to the wall and have to start all over again. If you catch Grandmother you take her place. The game is best played with no speaking apart from Grandmother.

Once the company become skilled at this then a variation is added. A bottle is placed behind Grandmother. The purpose of the game is to steal the bottle without being caught and to get it to the back of the room, by passing it from one company member to another without being caught moving the bottle. This adds strategy to the exercise, and brings a whole new dimension into the game.

Push and Pull

The company work in pairs. They stand opposite each other across the room. There is an imagined rope between them. A becomes the puller and B the one being pulled. They then see if they can pull the person across the room by the imaginary rope. They have to decide where the rope is tied, for example it could be tied round the neck, the waist or the arm. The exercise is repeated, this time pushing the partner, but with space between them.

An Imaginary Battle

Using an imaginary weapon of their choice, pairs of actors discover how to react to the various blows. This helps to establish action and reaction, and how to time it.

COMBAT MOVES

Once the actors are warmed up and are confident in working with each other, various aspects of combat can be explored. Every move is 'cheated' so that the aggressor does not inflict the injury he pretends to, and it is the receiver that reacts to it by crying out or grimacing. The positioning of the bodies is essential so that the 'blow' is masked by the actors and the noise of the punch or slap is clearly heard, and there should be a reaction to it, either a sharp movement or a cry.

The Slap

The slap to the face can be effective and easy to accomplish. There are several safe ways of producing this, but the actors have to remain cool and controlled. The actor inflicting the slap stands with his back to the audience and just to one side of the person receiving it. He raises his right hand to the side so that the audience sees it and then directs it towards his opponent's cheek. On the cue he brings his hand down and claps his left hand in front of him. At the same time the opponent moves his head sharply to the right as if it has been hit and, gripping his left cheek with his left hand, he emits a cry. The suddenness of the attack with the noise of the slap and the cry convince the audience. Alternatively, the opponent can supply the slap or another member of the cast standing around, but it is better for the aggressor to have control of that.

Direct Slap on the Face

This is more difficult and unless expertly done can be very painful and cause lasting damage, such as a perforated eardrum. It requires enormous cool from the recipient not to anticipate the slap, and for the aggressor to use a very relaxed hand. It is a good idea for the actors to practise slapping their own hands

Slapping or hitting the chest.

with a very relaxed wrist, and even slapping their own cheeks to feel what it is like. The slap should have no follow-through by the person delivering it, and preferably done with the upstage hand. There is no doubt that there is some pain involved, and unless really well executed and artistically necessary, it should be avoided.

The Punch

As with the slap, the combatants never need to make physical contact, and careful placing can mask the supposed point of contact from the audience.

The right hook directed towards the jaw can be simulated in two ways. The aggressor coincides the thrust of the blow with a sharp open-handed slap or punch with his own left hand onto his own chest. This can be rehearsed with an imaginary partner.

Alternatively, the blow can be directed towards the partner's open hand, which is placed where the blow is supposed to land.

The uppercut is easy to mask, and in this case the one delivering the blow can use their other hand and the one being hit can give a good reaction. Similarly, with a blow to the solar plexus the perpetrator can either engage his own hand or thump his chest.

For a slap to the nose the aggressor holds the opponent's nose gently between the index and the middle finger, closes the fist and with the other hand slaps the top of his hand.

Hair Pulling

This can look very effective and is relatively simple to execute. The actor who is pulling the hair places a closed fist on his opponent's head who then reacts. The one having their hair pulled uses one or both hands to hold onto the wrist of the aggressor, as if trying to remove his hands, thus offering the necessary support for the aggressor to look as if he is dragging his opponent across the room.

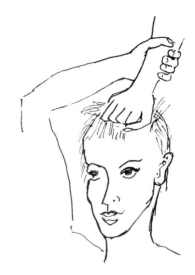

As if trying to remove his hands.

The Kick

There are a number of kicks, those delivered to an opponent on the floor, or a kick to the crutch. If the opponent is on the floor the aggressor kicks the floor and the receiver reacts.

The kick to the crutch can be like the slap to the face. It is violent and shocking. The kicker delivers a slapping blow to his opponent's hands which are extended as if for protection. A leather boot or shoe slapping the hand gives a good sound, and of course the receiver has a wonderful choice of reactions, horrific and often humorous at the same time.

Hitting the Head on a Door or Table

As for 'hair pulling' the aggressor takes his opponent towards the door or table with a clenched fist held on his opponent's head. The opponent places a free hand, palm down-wards, in front of his face and coincides the hitting of the head with a sharp slap on the door or table accompanied with the appropriate reaction. A similar effect can be made where it appears that the person has accidently walked into a closed door.

The kicker delivers a slapping blow.

The Half Nelson

This is an official way of restraining someone, where one arm is twisted round the back and pushed upwards, putting pressure on the shoulder joint. Again, this can work well if all the work is done by the one being restrained.

Blocking a Fight Sequence

I have indicated that a great deal of your production's movement can become the responsibility of the company working in small groups. You can use a similar technique with fights but you need to have done a lot of preparation. The fight needs to have a scenario, its own story. It has to have structure: a beginning, a middle and an end. It needs focus and rhythm, and these elements have to be planned beforehand. When the company are working in small groups, always make sure that a sensible and experienced member of the company is there as director, and that they work according to the rules established in the warm-up and the practising of the various moves. Don't let them experiment without proper supervision, and make sure that the groups are paired off into willing and sympathetic couples. It is often a good idea to give a nervous member an experienced and able partner to bring them on and give them confidence.

When rehearsing the fight sequence, as you begin to put all the elements together, divide the fight up into small units and rehearse them bit by bit, marking the movements, saving energy and allowing the company to see how and where their part of the fight takes place, and how it fits in with the rest of the company. In this way the focus will be easier to maintain, the dialogue will be heard and focused, and the whole thing will be controlled from the very beginning. Once the fight is set, it is essential to rehearse it every day, and also to run all or part of it before each performance, especially if you have doubly cast the play.

8   DEVISING YOUR OWN STORY OR PLAY

In this chapter let us look in more detail at some examples of devised pieces of theatre, adaptations from well known stories and journals. Let us start with storytelling. The basis of most drama is the story or narrative thrust. Some plays appear to have very little in the way of dramatic action. The plot is unravelled through the dialogue which slowly reveals a dramatic subtext, for instance the spirits that haunt Ibsen's play *Ghosts*. The orphanage does burn down, and Oswald falls in love with his half sister, but we only discover this as layer upon layer of the dead father's behaviour is peeled away. In a similar way J.B. Priestly's *Dangerous Corner* is an after-dinner conversation that develops into a thrilling exposure of passion and death, but this time the playwright plays with the element of time, but maintains a continuity of place, so in the end we are unsure about the truth, but have an insight into all the characters and what makes them tick. These two plays are examples of master playwrights working in a naturalistic style.

STORYTELLING

The above examples of plays will not be the kind of drama that your youth theatre will produce when it goes into creating its own version of a short story by the Brothers Grimm, like *The Fisherman and his Wife*. I suggest this story because it is concise, offers scope for drama and imagination and easily divides up into sections.

The difference between a dramatization and storytelling is the speed and agility with which the narration can move the story along. Earlier in the book I talked about the dramatic development of the plot and the epic or world in which the drama happens. This is more evident in storytelling. The company creates the epic themselves with their bodies, so that you do not need to have any scenery, or turn everything into dialogue, as the narration can be shared between the protagonists and the epic. Also if you show what is happening physically, it doesn't need to be explained vocally as well.

The story concerns a poor fisherman and his disgruntled wife, who live in a ditch by the seashore, until one day he catches a magic talking fish, who is in reality an enchanted prince. The fish promises to fulfil his every wish if the fisherman will release him. He frees the fish, goes home and tells his wife of the adventure. She tells her husband to ask for a cottage instead of the ditch they have as a home. He goes to the seashore, calls the fish who grants him his wish. The wife soon finds the cottage too small and demands better accommodation and thus starts a saga of greed and power, until she becomes King, Emperor, and eventually wants to command the whole world and the sun and moon, at which point the fish is no longer able to help her and they both return to the ditch for the rest of their days.

The Beginning

Let their first experience of the story be through the listening. Don't try to tell the story, just read it. Have a rehearsal at home, reading the story out loud, so that you become familiar with it. Place yourself in a good position, and use a chair, gathering the company around you, making sure that they are comfortable but not going to sleep on the floor. When the story has ended discuss their favourite moments. This can then lead into building up still pictures in small groups, and sharing the tableaux.

Developing the Dramatic Line

The next stage is to divide the company into groups with three or four people in each group. Give each group a part of the story to work on. *The Fisherman and his Wife* divides up well, but only give to each group that part of the story they are to work on. Ask them to choose some moments from their section of the story, and without using words create a series of tableaux that transform from one dramatic moment to another, as described in Chapter 6 when exploring scenes. We then see these tableaux in order. We get an idea of the development of the story. We see how the characters of the fish, the fisherman and his wife are perceived by each group. It is a good idea to observe the tableaux closely, choosing details that are interesting or even puzzling. This is good for the observers to develop clear precise language, and it also tests the integrity and stamina of the actors maintaining the tableau.

Telling the Story Using Language

Now let them repeat the exercise but this time they can use language, either their own words, or those lifted from the text they have been given. They need to find out how they use the narrative, and who speaks it. Do they each take a part and have the storyteller as a character on his or her own? Will they share narration and dialogue amongst the group? Do not let them use any props or furniture, and give them a limited time to create their part of the story. If they get through the work quickly and start over-rehearsing stop them. The scenes are then shared and we get another look at the story. Arrange them in a circle so that the story travels round the circle and there are no gaps, no applause or comment between one group and the next.

When they have finished sit them down and talk about the work, sharing observations. Discover what kind of a story it is, a romance, a thriller, or a moral tale. Before you leave this exercise get each group to write down what they performed. If it was improvised they should put down what they said, and how they organized it. They will need this later on.

Exploring the Epic

The next step is to consider the epic or the scenery, and the atmosphere of the story. A good exercise to start with is to use the whole group. They all have to create a still picture of say, a swimming pool, and then on your instruction bring it to life with sound and movement. With a crash on a cymbal, or a spoken signal they will freeze, and then create a busy railway terminus, a traffic jam, a state funeral. Gradually you can introduce scenes from the story. The fish coming to the surface of the sea for the first time: the beautiful little cottage: the wife sitting on her throne: the sea becoming angry. Don't allow them to think about it, but just do it. They have to work with each other and use their imaginations. They have to be in the picture, not looking on as a member of the audience. At this point they should not be judging themselves, and you are

Exploring the epic, students from GSA.

not judging them but giving them the freedom to express whatever they want within the scenario.

Giving Life to Inanimate Objects

From this exercise you can move quite freely into more specific and detailed work. Try all the places that are in the story, from the fisherman and his wife living in a ditch to the Emperor's Palace. As you look at each environment, encourage the actors to invest their tables and chairs, the beds and doors, the cupboards and refrigerators with character and what is more important, with a life. Does the bed like it when the Emperor lies on it? Is the cottage happy when the fisherman's wife becomes disgruntled with her surroundings and demands something better?

Putting the Dramatic and the Epic Together

You are now ready for the next step. Remember the earlier exercise when the groups took responsibility for a section of the story and showed it to the rest of the group and then wrote it down. They now return to their groups and their scripts. Let them have a

Working with a puppet.

look at their scripts and have a brief rehearsal. The whole group are now going to tell the story together. Those who have responsibility for the section will lead the section, become the characters and tell the story while the rest respond to the language, listen for what they need to do, and do it.

There is a great temptation to interfere if this exercise doesn't seem to be getting off the ground. Resist the temptation for it is only an exercise, and let them take the initiative. Some things might happen that take you by surprise

Improvisation

When creating a play, or discovering what lies behind the words and actions of a scene, the use of improvisation can be very useful. The actor will often experience an emotion or desire that they had been unable to find by just using the text. However, the way in which they express themselves can end up in a torrent of imprecise language. Some writer/directors, for example Mike Leigh, create all their plays and films not only through improvisation, but by a whole process of character work that takes weeks to perfect. The play is eventually written down almost verbatim but the actors who have created the words never see the script, they recall the play through being immersed in the action and their total identification with their character. This is a highly sophisticated way of working and should not be attempted unless you are very secure in your working methods. An improvisation should not be left hanging in the air, it needs to be secured in some way either by writing it down or using it as a stepping stone to enlighten the text, as is suggested in the 'text, improvised text' exercise in Chapter 6.

Improvising in pairs, Sheffield Youth Theatre.

and initially seem inappropriate, but be patient for it is their way of seeing the story, and if it is truthful and in the spirit of the original, let it happen. If, however, it is cheap and smart you will have to question people's choices.

The observations on the completion of this exercise are often crucial to the development of the group. The work will have a rough quality and there will be moments of inertia and lack of focus. These moments will be noticed and mentioned. There will also be moments of truth and beauty when the actors discover for the first time that they are transforming themselves from a raging sea storm into the towers and pinnacles of the Emperor's Palace and further finding out how they can all tell the story together.

You may need to try this exercise a second time if there has been confusion and reticence. But a conversation with words of constructive criticism and encouragement, will nearly always release the actors and if this happens at the end of a day's work it is good to send people home feeing they have achieved something rather than let themselves down.

The Trailer

Before moving on to the detailed work of structuring and writing down their version of the story, a fun and important exercise is for them to create the trailer, as described in Chapter 6.

Building the Story from the Beginning as a Group

We now come to the next step in the creation of their story. What previously has been loose and improvised now needs to be sharpened up. Roles have to be allocated, and language choices made and a script has to be written. The actors will have now gone through the story a number of times, each time with a different point of concentration.

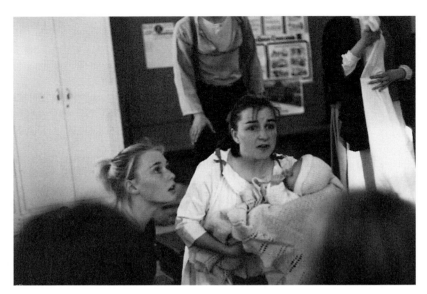

Sheffield Youth Theatre working on a scene built through improvisation.

The time has come to make some lists. We need a list of characters: a list of scenes, with a heading for each scene as to its dramatic development. In storytelling there has to be action to everything. Nothing stands still, everything moves, developing from one moment into another, and with the use of narration, or purely physically, we can change location and focus as the camera does in a film. As storytellers we have to establish with our audience what conventions we are going to use to tell our story.

Which Way Forward?

You now have two choices. Either you, a member of your support staff, or a writer who has been employed to create the final script, would now proceed with putting together all the work that has taken place during the devising process. There will need to be a gap in the proceedings for this to take place. The writer should have noted, recorded, or videotaped the important moment during the early rehearsals. There will also be the actor's

Cliques

Try to avoid the creation of cliques when working. People naturally like to form their own little group of friends and this is fine from a social point of view, but it doesn't help the work especially if the company's philosophy is based on friendship and equality. When the age range is wide the older company members need to help the younger ones when unravelling difficult texts. Shy members can feel very intimidated and a group of them working together all the time will not produce good work or create a good atmosphere. Keep your eyes open for the difficult or strong character who wants to dominate. It could be an excellent actor, but one whose ego and presence is not beneficial to the rest of the group, and he/she may have to go.

Creating Dialogue

If you are not used to writing dialogue, but have struggled to create a script that your company cannot bring to life, do not despair. If you have a structure, for instance the scene is between two brothers and sister arguing over a will, you could improvise it. Divide the company into groups of three people in each group, don't worry about what sex they are, and suggest where the scene should start, and where it needs to end up. The groups then improvise the scene. The many versions of the scene are then shared with the group, and after a discussion about what worked and what didn't, instruct them to go away and write the scene down. Collect all the versions and after the rehearsal you can amalgamate them. In such a way you can graft a lot of your play.

notes, their scripts and of course the words of the original transcript to draw upon for the finished product, and it should reflect all these elements.

The story script that will be given to the company for the final stages of rehearsals should contain all the words that need to be spoken, and the actors should be able to recognize their work now organized into a complete text.

The other journey puts a heavy responsibility on the ensemble. The company would have to go through the same process as above, but do it as a company. Your scene breakdown list will be your guide. Allocate one or two people to take responsibility for each scene, they will then act as director or writer, and will stand outside the action to report back to the rest of the group what is happening and what needs to be done. Their place in the action will be kept for them, so it is

better if it is someone who does not have a major role in the story at that time. This puts an enormous responsibility on the group but it does help them to become very involved in the creative process. The job of the director during this period of work is merely to observe and not to interfere unless asked to. Your assessment of the work produced at the end of this process, however, is very important. Your taste and experience will be needed so that the story will be suited to its audience. The process of shaping the final product, will call upon your skill as a director.

AN EXAMPLE OF HOW TO CREATE A SCENE OUT OF A PIECE OF NARRATIVE

The following extracts are from *Rural Rides* by William Cobbett. It is part of an entry made in the journal on 20 October 1825. This was the source material used for a scene in a play devised and presented by the Sheffield Youth Theatre in the 1980s and revived in 2003. The scene is just part of a whole play that was a collage of writing created during a two-week period. I had the privilege of being part of the team that developed the material and was also the editor/writer. The material was divided up into sections, and given to four groups.

Section One

Having done my business at Hartswood to-day about eleven o'clock, I went to a sale at a farm, which the farmer is quitting. Here I had a view of what has been going on all over the country. The farm, which belonged to Christ's Hospital, has been held by a man of the name of Charington, in whose family the lease has been, I hear, a great number of years . . . Everything about this farmhouse, was formerly the scene of plain manners and plentiful living. Oak clothes chests, oak bed-steads, oak chests of drawers, and oak table to eat on, long, strong, and well supplied with joint stools. Some of the things were many hundreds of years old. But all appeared to be in a state of decay and nearly disuse. There appeared to have been hardly any family in that house, where formerly there were in all possibility, from ten to fifteen men, boys, and maids: and, which was worst of all, there was a parlour! Aye, and a carpet and bell pull too! One end of the front of this once plain and substantial house had been moulded into 'a parlour;' and there was a mahogany table, and the fine chairs, and the fine glass, and all as bare-faced upstart as any stock-jobber in the kingdom can boast of. And, there were the decanters, the glasses, the 'dinner set' of crockery ware, and all just in the true stock jobber style. And I dare say it has been 'Squire Charington and the Miss Charingtons; and not plain Master Charington, and his son Hodge and his daughter Betty Charington, all of whom this accursed system has, in all likelihood, transmuted into a species of mock gentlefolks, while it has ground the labourers down into real slaves.

Section Two

Why do not farmers now feed and lodge their work people, as they did formerly? Because they cannot keep them upon so little as they give them in wages. This is the real cause of the change. There needs no more to prove that the lot of the working classes has become worse than it formerly was. This fact alone is sufficient to settle this point. All the world knows, that a number of people, boarded in the same house, and at the same table, can, with as good food, be boarded cheaper than those persons divided into twos, threes, or fours, can be boarded. This is a well-known truth: therefore, if the farmer now shuts his pantry against his labourers, and pays them wholly in money, is it not clear, that he does it because he thereby gives then a living cheaper

to him; that is to say, a worse living than formerly? Mind he has a house for them; a kitchen for them to sit in, bedrooms for them to sleep in, tables, and stools, and benches, of everlasting duration. All these he has; all these cost him nothing; and yet so much does he gain by pinching them in wages that he lets all these things remain as of no use, rather than feed labourers in the house. Judge, then, of the change that has taken place in the condition of these labourers! And, be astonished, if you can, at the pauperism and the crimes that now disgrace this once happy and moral England.

Section Three

The land produces, on an average, what it always produced; but, there is a new distribution of the produce. This 'squire Charington's father used, I dare say, to sit at the head of the oak-table along with his men, say grace to them, and cut up the meat and the pudding. He might take a cup of strong beer to himself, when they have none; but, that was pretty nearly all the difference in their manner of living. So that all lived well. But, the 'squire had many wine decanters and wine glasses and a 'dinner set', and a 'breakfast set', and 'desert knives', and these evidently imply carryings on and a consumption that must of necessity have greatly robbed the long oak table if it remained fully tenanted. That long table could not share in the work of the decanters and the dinner set. Therefore, it became almost untenanted; the labourers retreated to hovels, called cottages; and, instead of boards and lodging, they got money; so little of it as to enable the employer to drink wine; but, then, that he might not reduce them to quite starvation, they were enabled to come to him, in the king's name, and demand food as paupers. And, now, mind, that which a man receives in the king's name, he knows well he has by force; and it is not in the nature that he should thank any body for it, and least of all the party from whom it is forced. Then, if this sort of force be insufficient to obtain him enough to eat and keep him warm, is it surprising, if he think it no great offence against God (who created no man to starve) to use another sort of force more within his own control? Is it, in short, surprising, if he resort to theft and robbery?

Section Four

I could not quit this farm-house without reflecting on the thousands of scores of bacon and thousands of bushels of bread that had been eaten from the long oak-table, which, I said to myself, is now perhaps, going, at last, to the bottom of a bridge that some stock-jobber will stick up over an artificial river in his rockery garden. 'By- it shant,' said I, almost in a real passion: and so I requested a friend to buy it for me; and if he do so, I will take it to Kensington, or to Fleet Street, and keep it for the good it has done the world.

When the old farm-houses are down (and down they must come in time) what a miserable thing the country will be! Those that are now erected are mere painted shells, with a Mistress within, who is stuck up in a place she calls a parlour, with, if she have children, the 'young ladies and gentlemen' about her: some showy chairs and a sofa (a sofa by all means): half a dozen prints in guilt frames hanging up: some swinging book-shelves with novels and tracts upon them: a dinner brought in by a girl that is perhaps better 'educated' than she: two or three nick-nacks to eat instead of a piece of bacon and a pudding: the house too neat for a dirty shoed carter to be allowed to come into; and everything proclaimed to every single beholder, that there is here a constant anxiety to make a show not warranted by the reality. The children (which is the worst part of it) are too clever to work: they are all to be gentlefolks. Go to plough! Good God! What, young 'gentlemen' go to plough! They become

clerks, or some skinny-dish thing or other. They flee from the dirty work as cunning horses do from the bridle. What misery is all this! What a mass of materials for producing that general and dreadful convulsion that must, first or last, come and blow this funding and jobbing and enslaving and starving system to atoms!

EXPLORING THE TEXT

Each group allocated a scribe who had the responsibility of recording who was in the group and kept a record of any lists or important discoveries that the group might make. The first task was for them to read the text to each other aloud around the group and share as much as they could remember. Any words they did not understand were looked up in a dictionary, but the temptation to give them quick glib answers was resisted.

The exploration of their extracts followed similar investigations described in the storytelling, lists of character explicit and implicit were made; scenes that were described or hinted at were listed; the objects that appeared in the scenes were also noted down.

CREATING TABLEAUX

Following this investigation a series of tableaux were produced, each group finding contrasting moments in their section. The tableaux were held for a long time so that the other groups could examine them in detail. If you have space and can work in separate rooms, it can be very exciting for the group showing their tableaux to get into position in their room before the other groups enter. The visitors then describe what they see. It should be prefixed by the phrase 'I see . . .' which is then followed for example by . . ., 'two opposite classes projecting two different personalities'. Or another comment was, 'Rich and poor

Sheffield Youth Theatre sharing their explorations as a group.

turning backs. What would happen if they turned round to face each other?' Prefixing the observation slightly formalized the language. The scribe needs to write down these comments.

Another way of encouraging some language is for someone to stand behind one of the still characters or a piece of furniture in the room, and speak for it, similar to the exercise, giving life to inanimate objects, described earlier in this chapter. All the sections were looked at. Sometimes the company for one reason or another lost focus and concentration but an appeal to their integrity and a brief relaxation in the tableaux renewed energy and relieved a locked elbow, a stiff knee, or a watery eye.

A WRITING EXERCISE

Once all the groups' work had been seen and investigated a writing exercise followed. If you have plenty of space available, have pieces of paper, pencils or pens laid out in a separate room. An invitation to move into another room where everything is laid out for them to do some writing, helps them to use a different part of themselves, making the shift from performer to playwright, but without losing focus or the atmosphere and involvement of the preceding exercise. They were given ten to fifteen minutes to write from the point of view of a character or a piece of furniture. It had to be in the first person, and about the inner thoughts of the character or object. We told them to put the pen to the paper and let it do

Sharing a scene that has just been written.

the writing, as described in Chapter 2. When it is finished everyone needs to put the name of their character on the piece of paper, and it is collected for future use. The following extracts were the result of this exercise:

Young Master Charington: 'I wonder why father has to dismiss the old man. He is a good friend of mine. He used to take me up the river fishing. I've seen him bag many a deer and countless rabbits. He mustn't see me looking . . . I'll look away. I can't believe father is going to ruin a man's life, just for the sake of a cabbage.'

Betty: 'Perhaps he will talk to me. Yes that would be best if he talked to me. I want so much to be part of his group, his friends. The way they go off together. Oh! I know I have my job, I have my friends, but to be with him would be so much better, much, much better.'

The actors who wrote these little monologues had other experiences to draw on. Not just from the section they were studying but a variety of acting exercises some of which you will find in Chapter 6, and of course other extracts from Cobbett's journals. The company also created their own country dances. There are a number of historical dances that you can teach the company. The Farandole, a Brawl, or Strip the Willow, are all social dances, that are easy to learn and can be used as a framework for transforming from one scene into another.

PUTTING IT ALL TOGETHER

Using parts of the extract from the journal, the scene that follows was written after the creative workshop process was completed. There were a few days between the workshop period and the rehearsals that allowed me to edit and organize the actors' work into the play. Because it was their work the rehearsals that followed were comparatively straight-forward as the scenes and dialogue were familiar, since they had already explored them, and the language was a mixture of Cobbett's, their own, and occasionally mine. The scene that follows was the result of the work done during the creative period, and was performed

113

Rural Rides, *the Farmhouse dance.*

Watching a scene.

by the company. The director cast a number of actors as Cobbett, and a band was created out of the company, led by a local folk musician.

The Farmhouse.

COBBETT: Having done my business at Hartswood to-day about eleven o'clock, I went to a sale at a farm, which the farmer is quitting. Here I had a view of what has been going on all over the country. The farm, which belonged to Christ's Hospital, has been held by a man named Charington.

Charington Appears.

In whose family the lease has been, I hear, a great number of years . . . Everything about this farmhouse, was formerly the scene of plain manners and plentiful living.

Harvest Dance Starts. The Old Charingtons Arrive.

Oak clothes chests, oak bed-steads, oak chests of drawers, and oak table to eat on, long strong, and well supplied with joint stools. This Squire Charington's father used, I dare say to sit at the head of the oak table along with his men . . . say grace to them.

Master Charington: For what we are about to receive, may the Lord make us truly thankful.

Cobbett: And cut up the meat and pudding.

The Supper Starts

Voice One: The loud clatter of voices doesn't echo on the walls, it sinks into the oak furniture and adds an extra warmness to the room. The food is good. I'm surprised to see the farmer and his wife are eating the same as me and my husband.

Another Labourer: He sits at one end of the table with his family. The rest of us all together forgetting our worries and aching limbs . . . for tonight anyway.

Harvest Dance then the Picture Freezes.

Cobbett: Some of the things were many hundreds of years old. But all appeared to be in a state of decay and nearly disuse. There appeared to have been hardly any family in that house. . . And, which is the worst of all, a parlour had been added.

The Wall: I am the beautifully decorated wall. I separate the people inside from the people outside. Were I not here, they, they would all be the same.

Picture: I am a beautiful picture of a young woman in a garden. I've been hanging on this wall for a long time and I'm bored. I feel ashamed to hang on these walls. We are not used or treated with respect. Our purpose is solely to be admired by their friends.

Sofa: They call me a sofa but really I'm not made for sitting on. People perch on the end of me, feeling awkward and making polite conversation. I won't last long, even though I look showy and expensive.

Cobbett: And I dare say it has been. . .

Squire Charington: Squire Charington.

Miss Charingtons: And the Miss Charingtons.

Young Master Charington: And young Master Charington.

Cobbett: And not. . .

Master Charington: Plain Master Charington.

Hodge: And his son Hodge.

Betty: And his daughter Betty, sitting at this table watching family and friends eat this meal I feel satisfied knowing it's me who has prepared it for their enjoyment.

Master Charington: My! They are enjoying themselves tonight. It's been a good year, a fine harvest and good weather.

Greedy Woman: Shall I have potatoes or green beans?

Cobbett: Why do not farmers now feed and lodge their work people, as they did formerly? Because they cannot keep them upon so little as they give them in wages.

The Parlour – an Old Man Enters in Silence and is Ordered out.

Voice One: Look! Over there in the Parlour.

Voice Two: It's an old man in ragged clothes.

Voice Three: He seems out of place.

Voice Four: What does he want?

Voice One: I wonder why the old man is being asked to leave?

Voice Two: I wonder if the hand on the shoulder is comforting or forcing.

Voice Three: Is he being asked to leave?

Voice One: Or having something pointed out to him?

Voice Three: Is she pointing to the shoes of the old man?

Voice Two: Perhaps the old man's left footmarks.

First Miss Charington: Look at this old fool! Look at his muddy shoes! What a disgrace! What an embarrassment!

Second Miss Charington: Oh leave the old man alone. He hasn't done anything wrong. He just didn't agree with your methods of farming and after all he was right. He didn't mean to take those vegetables. He didn't have enough money to feed his family.

Cobbett: All the world knows, that a number of people, boarded in the same house, and at the same table, can, with as good food, be boarded cheaper than those persons divided into twos, threes, or fours, can be boarded. This is a well-known truth: therefore, if the farmer now shuts his pantry against his labourers, and pays them wholly in money, is it not clear, that he does it because he thereby gives them a living cheaper to him; that is to say, a worse living than formerly?

Back to the Harvest Supper.

Greedy Woman: No! I think green beans.

Labourer: I look forward to this every year. It's good to see a year's work on the table, in front of you.

Hodge: I'm Hodge, and I'm sitting here amongst most of my father's friends. The feast stares me in the face, as though I shouldn't touch it.

Another Labourer: This is one of the few times I and master really talk.

Betty Charington Serving Food Behind a Young Man.

Betty: Perhaps he will talk to me. Yes that

would be best if he talked to me. I want so much to be part of his group, his friends. The way they go off together. Oh! I know I have my job, I have my friends, but to be with him would be so much better, much, much better. Because then I would be someone. What can I say to him, to give me a place in his company? How should I present myself to him to make him take me into his company?

The Harvest Dancers Whirl Her Away with Him into a Wedding Dance. The Parlour.

Young Master Charington: I wonder why father has to dismiss the old man. He is a good friend of mine. He used to take me up the river fishing. I've seen him bag many a deer and countless rabbits. He mustn't see me looking . . . I'll look away. I can't believe father is going to ruin a man's life, just for the sake of a cabbage.

Cobbett: Mind he has a house for them; a kitchen for them to sit in, bedrooms for them to sleep in, tables, and stools, and benches, of everlasting duration. All these he has; all these cost him nothing; and yet so much does he gain by pinching them in wages that he lets all these things remain as of no use, rather than feed labourers in the house.

Greedy Woman: No! Potatoes.

Voice One: Clatter of voices.

Betty: Meat.

Master Charington: Pudding.

Labourer: Ale.

Voice Two: Oak furniture.

Labourer: Green beans.

Labourer: Bread.

Voice Three: Extra warmness.

Labourer: Cheese

Labourer: Oatcake

Labourer: Butter.

Labourer: Chew.

Labourer: Squash.

Labourer: Tear.

Labourer: Cheese.

Labourer: Chew.

Labourer: Squash.

Voices: The dusty smell of corn hangs in the room. The smell of harvest time.

To the Parlour.

Voice One: I remember a few years ago it was harvest time.

Voice Two: I used to play with his children.

Voice Three: Why has everything changed?

Squire Charington: Out! Get out!

Voice Four: I remember when he took us for walks through the cornfields.

Voice One: If you had given him enough wages in the first place he wouldn't have had to steal.

117

Old Man: I've lived here since you were born.

Squire Charington: Out!

**The Old Man Goes.
As He Leaves the Harvest Supper Follow
Him. Only Master Charington's Family
and the Squire's Family Remain.**

Cobbett: I could not quit this farm-house without reflecting on the thousands of scores of bacon and thousands of bushels of bread that had been eaten from the long oak-table, which, I said to myself, is now perhaps, going, at last, to the bottom of a bridge that some stock-jobber will stick up over an artificial river in his rockery garden.

**The People on the Stage Reflect the
Voices.**

Voice One: I see two opposite classes projecting two different personalities.

Voice Two: Perhaps it is the past and the present.

Voice Three: Perhaps the servant and the master.

Voice Four: I don't know if I see a good side and a bad one.

Voice One: Perhaps one side is reality. The other is illusion.

Voice Two: Perhaps it is the proper and the preferable.

Voice Three: Perhaps it is the outer and the inner man.

Voice One: I see these people seeing things as they have to do it.

Voice Two: The heads are down on this side, up on the other.

Voice Three: One leaning on the other, like a see-saw.

Voice One: Can it change?

Voice Four: One day it will change.

Voice Three: One side is resting on the ground.

Voice Two: The other side up in the air.

Voice Four: Each desires to be what the other is.

All: Rich and poor turning backs. What would happen if they turned round to face each other?

**Whispered Voices and Shadows of
Harvesters.**

Harvesters: We plant the seeds together.
We helped things grow together.
We gathered the harvest together.
We prepared the food together.
We eat together.
We are one body.
We are equal.

One Voice: Well at least for today, anyway.

**Back in the Parlour just the Children
and the Furniture. Silence.**

One Voice: The children are like the furniture, hard and fine on the outside, but soft underneath.

The Adults Join the Children.

Cobbett: When the old farm-houses are down (and down they must come in time) what a miserable thing the country will be! Those that are now erected are mere painted shells, with a Mistress within, who is stuck up in a place she calls a parlour, with, if she have children, the 'young ladies and gentlemen' about her: some showy chairs and a sofa (a sofa by all means): half a dozen prints in guilt frames hanging up: some swinging book-shelves with novels and tracts upon them: a dinner brought in by a girl that is perhaps better 'educated' than she: two or three nick-nacks to eat instead of a piece of bacon and a pudding: the house too neat for a dirty shoed carter to be allowed to come into; and everything proclaimed to every single beholder, that there is here a constant anxiety to make a show not warranted by the reality. The children (which is the worst part of it) are too clever to work: they are all to be gentlefolks. Go to plough! Good God! What, young 'gentlemen' go to plough! They become clerks, or some skinny-dish thing or other. They flee from the dirty work as cunning horses do from the bridle. What misery is all this! What a mass of materials for producing that general and dreadful convulsion that must, first or last, come and blow this funding and jobbing and enslaving and starving system to atoms!

This scene concluded the first half of the play. If you are seriously considering creating you own piece of theatre make sure that you

Dress rehearsal of **Rural Rides,** *Sheffield Youth Theatre.*

organize your time. The company becomes the corporate writer during the creative period. Leave enough time after this period is over to edit, write, and structure the whole thing. If you have been true to the creative process and are using the company's own language the rehearsal period should not produce any problems. Be disciplined, keep to deadlines and trust your creative judgement. Type the script out clearly for the beginning of the rehearsal period, and treat the play with the respect it deserves. Do not be drawn into making little changes here and there, but if you sense that something isn't working take the proper action to rectify it. It may be a simple question of reordering some of the material or making a simple cut. Make sure that the technical team are informed about any changes that have taken place during the creative and rehearsal process.

9 THE TECHNICAL AND DRESS REHEARSALS

Your production is now into the final stages with the crucial transition from rehearsal into performance. Excitement and nerves make this a tricky time for everyone. As Director you will be concerned with the technical aspects of the production, and you will have to leave your cast in order to attend the lighting rehearsals, the organizing of the sets and costumes, the sale of tickets and programmes. The front-of-house manager will want to know how long the play will run, and whether you want the seats to be numbered. It is important that you have an assistant or co-director at this time so that the actors are not left stranded. It needs to be someone who has seen them through some of the rehearsal period, has won their trust and respect, and is a calming influence who can focus their attention and keep them out of mischief.

The actors are now confronted with a conventional stage and its complicated system of lighting, and with the audience sitting in the dark, which is a far cry from the security of the rehearsal room that has been the actor's home for the last three weeks. Even if you are still in your own school, the space chosen for the performances could be in a different part of the campus, and the cast will not have seen or worked on the finished set. There will have to be final costume fittings and a possible dress parade, and with the date of the first performance looming organization and timing are of the essence. All these things have to happen over a weekend, or if you are lucky it could be a week. Let us look at a weekend starting on a Saturday morning. This would fit into a production going on in a school or local hall. If your production was opening in the local theatre or community hall, work would not start until Sunday morning.

THE GET-IN

This refers to bringing all the requirements for the production into the theatre or performing space. It includes the scenery, any extra lighting equipment, the costumes and props. Some equipment might have been delivered earlier and that should have been looked after by the theatre's resident Stage Manager. Arrange your transport so that it knows where to pick up everything and where it needs to go. Make sure that your Production Manager has done this; that there is adequate staff arranged to help load and unload the equipment; that the various places know the time of arrival and that you have access (keys, etc) or that your hosts are expecting you, the building is unlocked and you know the way to the 'get in'. In most theatres this will not be where the audience enter but somewhere at the back and approached by a different street.

Unless told otherwise by the resident Stage Manager, bring everything onto the fore stage and before you do anything else check that it is all there. It is a good idea to label boxes and skips (large baskets for carrying costumes) so that they can be taken to their destinations.

THE WARDROBE AND COSTUMES

If there isn't a separate wardrobe, designate a room where all the costumes are to be taken. The wardrobe staff will organize the setting up of an iron and sewing machine. They will have organized hangers and large draw-string bags for each actor (to hold their shoes, socks, shirts and costume accessories). The dressing rooms are usually allocated by the stage manager, but the wardrobe staff will arrange them with labelled chairs or pegs for each actor. There will still be a multitude of things to do, costumes to finish and press, shoes to dye, and hems to take up. Sensible wardrobe assistants are very useful, so are friendly parents who are often willing to be involved. A happy, calm wardrobe can be a wonderful refuge during

Mid-technical, the wardrobe sorts out accessories.

Costume waiting to be fitted.

these stressful days, where a kind word and a cup of tea can do wonders.

FIRST AID

Decide where your First-Aid Box will be kept and who will be in charge of it.

PROPS

It is important to have a responsible person in charge of the props and he or she will need to have a special place to unpack and keep them safe. Some plays will have lots of props. A big musical for instance may have masks, parasols and fans which are used by the chorus. These will all need to be taken care of and returned after use to *the Prop Table*.

This is a table where all the props are placed at the beginning of each performance. The table is marked off into sections for each prop which can then be checked with the prop list. This job can be carried out by a member of the cast or can be one of your stage management helpers who do not want to perform. They will take great pride in their props as they may have made some of them, or spent precious hours looking for them, and persuading someone to lend them for the length of the production.

Sometimes the property master will have responsibility for the furniture as well.

A props plot for each scene will also have to be made. This will show where all the furniture and all the props are set. Before the performance starts the props person can then check what is to be set with the list. It is also the responsibility of the props people to maintain the props during the run of the play, mending those that have been broken, rewriting letters that are torn up during the action of the play and locking up firearms after they have been used.

THE SET

In Chapter 5 we learnt a lot about the set. If you have a designer he or she will take responsibility for the erecting of it. If you are in a sophisticated theatre with a fly tower and

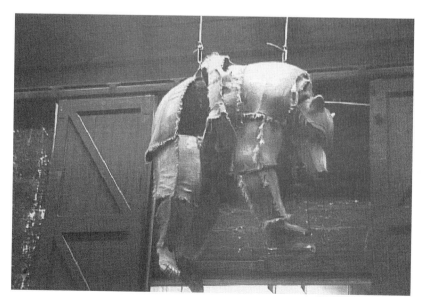

No room on the prop table – the bear has to be flown.

counterweight grid system, it will be necessary to fly some pieces of scenery and attach special lights to some of the bars reserved for the lights. These things have to done in the early stages of the fit-up, so make sure it is all in order.

MARKING UP

Measuring and marking out where things will go on the stage floor is important, so your ground plan drawn to scale will come in useful. The positioning and angle of the lights have to coincide with your set, and the set has to fit into the stage area so that all the exits and entrances work and there is enough space for the action to take place.

SCENE PLOTS

Whichever type of seating arrangement you have chosen for your production, or if you are performing in a conventional theatre, make sure that the backstage area is well organized. Someone has to work out where everything will live, so that once you have finished with a

Firearms Licence

If your production requires the use of a firearm that has to fire blank cartridges during the production, you will have to hire a suitable weapon and get a Firearms Licence from the local police station.

piece of scenery it has its special place backstage. If left anywhere it could be hiding a truck you may need at the end of the play. There may be so many scenes and so much scenery that you have to remove some of it at the interval into another place in order to make room for the next act. Simple plans of each setting can be photocopied and put at various places backstage so that your stage crew will be able to check what they have to do before each scene change.

The Stage Crew

The stage crew is responsible for changing the scenery at all the dress rehearsals and at each

A prop bookcase.

Student carpenter building the furniture.

The finished desk at the fit-up.

performance. It is important to organize continuity in personnel. Have a person in charge of stage right and stage left, and make sure that everyone is allocated specific jobs, so that someone taking off a chair, for instance, does not collide with two people bringing on a bed. Remember that these scene changes have to be rehearsed, in order for them to be swift, silent and efficient. The pre-planning of this is essential, so make sure that if you have a Stage Director he will know that this is his responsibility. Once the backstage area is filled with a large cast of actors, and it is dark, accidents can happen. Noise and chatter can disturb what is happening on the stage and interfere with the actor's concentration, and may even be audible to the audience.

125

		Production Schedule Once a Catholic	
Date	Time	Event	Called
Sun 20/10	10–1	LX Re-rig/Auditorium change round	SD; AP; ET; NG; RW; IW; HG; CH
	1–2	Lunch	
	2–6	Fit-up commences LX Rig FOH	
	6–7	Supper	
	7–10 10pm	Finish fit up Call ends	
Mon 21/10	9.30am	LX Focus commences	SD; HG; OJ; MH
	1–2	Lunch	
	2–6	LX Focus continues Prop get in	AP;RW
	6–7	Supper	
	7–10.30 10.30pm	LX Plot Call ends	HGi; SW to join
Tuesday 22/10	9am 9.30am 10–1	Crew call for technical Cast Call for tech Technical Rehearsal Commences	Show Crew ET; NG; Full Cast SW to join
	1–2	Lunch	
	2–5.30	Technical continues	
	5.30–6.30	Supper	
	6.55pm	Half Hour Call	Full Company
	7.30pm	Dress Rehearsal 1	

Production schedule for Once a Catholic.

LIGHTING

The hanging and focusing of the lights will be happening at the same time as the building of the set. Co-operation between the two departments is essential to make sure that everything happens smoothly. In some modern theatres the lighting is very sophisticated with a computerized board and lamps that can tilt, rotate and change colour at the touch of a button. To visualize this, consider the effects that can be achieved at a rock concert, where the lights are synchronized with the music. In your school hall you may have hardly any equipment at all and only the basic access to power. Find out from an official source that you are not going to overload the system and cause either a massive power failure or a fire.

Stage Lighting
This is serviced by different kinds of lamps:

The Flood
This can be placed on the ground or on a stand and has a reflector at the back. A flood will cover a large area with light and is used for lighting backing flats and areas of the stage and setting. Smaller versions of the flood are joined together in battens which are used to light the bottom of backcloths or as *footlights* at the very front of the stage. A similar line of lamps but that are hung from above the stage are called *battens*. It is possible to put coloured filters (*gels*) in these lamps that will alter the atmosphere and the colour of the set, producing a sunrise, a sunset, or the beginnings of a storm.

The Acting Area Flood
This is suspended from above the acting area and produces a pool of more concentrated light. *A pageant* is a lamp without a lens but the bulb can move in relation to the reflector that will affect the width of the beam. This is useful to give the effect of sunlight through a window.

A spotlight is a lamp that not only has a reflector but also a lens so that it produces a concentrated beam of light. It comes in many sizes and is usually linked with a similar lamp, in pairs. It can also be coloured with a gel. The spot bar is usually made up of a series of different spots and is hung towards the front of the stage. Other lamps are situated in the front of house and angled in such a way that they will not cause shadows on the backcloth.

The Function of Lighting
Lighting enables the audience to see the performers clearly, and helps them to focus on

Various floods, spotlights and a lighting board.

the heart of the drama. It should also add atmosphere to the production, and enhance the design. There is a great art to lighting design and some of the best in the profession can command huge salaries.

To light an actor successfully on the stage you will need to have more than one lamp focused on them. A young and inexperienced cast have enough to think about without constantly trying to 'find their light'. Also when time is running short, too many cues, merely for effect, can hold up a technical or dress rehearsal. So if you are not blessed with talent or wonderful equipment it is safer to err on the side of simplicity.

Try to avoid too many blackouts, especially if you have a lot of people on the stage or a lot more waiting to enter.

Hang and position the lamps bearing in mind how and where you are going to bring the electric supply to them. Once you have hung the lamps they need to be focused and coloured. To use just the bare light can be very unattractive for the actors and the scenery, so the lamps may need to be softened with a delicate colour or a frost which will just take the hard edge off the lamp. Be careful of shadows being cast on the backcloth and the flats, and always get a member of the stage management to 'walk' for you. This should be someone who knows where all the actors have to be in each scene so that you can see whether they will be lit. You should not be aware of any shadows or darker areas as they move across the stage

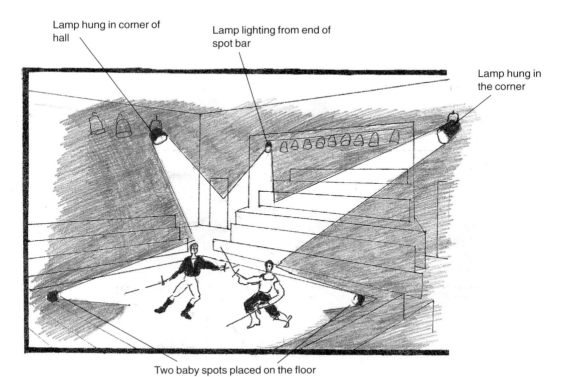

Lamp hung in corner of hall

Lamp lighting from end of spot bar

Lamp hung in the corner

Two baby spots placed on the floor

How to light a thrust or 'in-the-round' format.

Slides and Gobos

These can be used to great effect as was mentioned in Chapter 5. Just remember that a shape created by a light will only remain effective if the rest of the lighting is at a low level. This could work well for the marriage of Romeo and Juliet where there are only four characters present, but if it were the marriage of Hero and Claudio in *Much Ado about Nothing* you would need a lot more light, as there are many more characters in the scene.

Plotting the Lights

Sound and lighting plots are covered earlier in the book, and in the planning stages the Director and Lighting Designer may have worked out every cue, but you will now need to go through them again, first to see how it looks and also to allow the Deputy Stage Manager to write them down in the Book (prompt copy), and where they happen in the action. Many theatres have computerized boards, but make sure that the board operator also writes down every cue on a cue sheet in detail – that is, which lamps are being used and at what level. This is in case you have a computer failure in the middle of a performance and all the cues are lost and the board has to be worked manually.

The transition from one cue to another can be done in many ways – for example, a *fade* in which the lights dim or increase at a selected speed. A *cross fade* happens when one set of lights dims as the other comes up, sometimes at different speeds. A *blackout* is when all the lights snap out, and a *snap on* when all the lights come up. A *follow on* is when some lights will slowly come on after a main cue is given. Each cue has to be given a number starting with Cue 1 and working consecutively through the play – for example, *Elecs cue 1*.

GIVING THE CUES

It is important for the DSM to know when the light cues need to be given. Some will be a matter of common sense, for instance once the scene is set and the stage manager clears the stage, or simultaneously with the curtain going up. On the other hand the lighting cues could always follow the actions of the actors, which means that the timing will always be slightly different every performance. Another motivation for cues could be the music, especially in a musical or opera.

THE SOUND

Depending upon your production and whether it has a simple or complicated sound plot, you will have to go through a similar process as with the lighting. Some of the sound effects will have been pre-recorded on a *tape*, others may be created live. Make sure that the tapes are edited with coloured leader between each cue and also with metal stops to prevent the cues overrunning. The sound system will have various speakers placed around the stage and you will have to decide from which speaker the sound will come. You can achieve some very spectacular effects with a stereo system, but again beware of being too smart, and make sure that the sound is well recorded and enhances the atmosphere rather than destroys it. You will need to have a sound plotting session, where the levels and the speakers are decided upon and the cues marked down on the *sound plot* and also in the Book. Each cue has to be given a number starting with Cue 1 and working consecutively through the play as with the lights. Sound cues are usually marked as Fx – for example, *Fx cue 1*.

It is possible to work with two tapes so that cross fading can be achieved, or one tape can carry the atmosphere, a jungle for instance, and the other player the different sound effects that can be brought in on cue. Once the

Rob Wells   Page 2

Cabaret Act 1   FOLLOW SPOT 'Q' SHEET

FSQ	LXQ	COL	IRIS	ACTION	NOTES
—	60	O/w	Sm	Shmis face	behind Sheet
14 A	61	\	\	fade off as they exit	
15	64	frost 205	med	Shmder	SL
15 A	68	\	\	Slow fade out	
16	—	frost	med	Clip slow fade in	Table → bed
16 A	78	\	\	Slow fade out	
17	79	O/w	face	Shmi snap up	
17 1	84	"	med	Slow move in	
17.2	85	"	½	snap out large	
18 A	86	\	\	snap	
20	89	frost	Sm	Shmder	SL
20 A	91	\	\	Very slow fade	
21	97	frost 205	med	Scholts	DSL
21 A	98	\	\	Slow fade out	
22	99	frost 202	med	Koart	CS
22 A	101	\	\	Slow fade	
23	103	O/w	med	As Shmi rises	CS
23 A	104	\	\	snap out	

Follow spot cue sheet for **Cabaret.**

audience are seated the sound becomes muffled so be careful to *set your levels a notch higher*. Rehearse off-stage noises at the technical rehearsal.

MUSICALS

A band call will be necessary if your play is a musical or has live music. If there is only a pianist who has attended most of the rehearsals then a short *voice and singing warm up* will be needed before the technical. If, however, a bigger orchestra is being used then you will need to have a band call. This doesn't need to happen on the stage or in the pit but can be somewhere else. The orchestra will need to practise the score with the Musical Director, and then later to have a rehearsal with the actors and singers.

THE TECHNICAL REHEARSAL

You should now be ready for the first rehearsal that we will call the *Technical* when all the above elements are put together, bit by bit, including the actors. Some directors like to cut to cue. This can be confusing.

If the setting is a permanent structure and you have the time, it can be useful to *let the actors have a run of the play on the set* without the lights and costumes. This will allow them to get used to the new space and begin to make it their own, to find their way around backstage with the working lights and to try out any changes. It will allow them to find out about the acoustics of the theatre, to explore the auditorium as well as the stage, to talk to each other in pairs, one on the stage and another in a part of the auditorium so they can sense where they have to send the story.

Pre-Technical Pep Talk

Before anything is done, gather all the company together to make sure that every-body remembers the credo that was agreed on at the very first rehearsal. Point out the need for adult and disciplined behaviour, and make sure that you have someone in authority backstage whose sole job is to keep the company in a quiet state of readiness.

MAKE-UP

Make-up should be used with discretion, if at all. Young faces plastered with rouge, lipstick and blue or green eye-shadow, can look rather obscene, and the whole function of make-up is to bring out the features, and give a uniform look to the cast so that they appear to come from the same world. You might find it necessary to apply a light base, and some colour to the cheeks, but heavy lines and shadows for those playing older characters should be avoided at all costs. The hairstyles should be appropriate to the character and facial hair carefully applied, if a beard or moustache is required. Some firms will make up sideburns, moustaches and beards to order but they cost money. Crêpe hair can be purchased in various colours and comes in skeins. It has to teased out and flattened out between damp cloths, and applied with spirit gum.

A COSTUME PARADE

If most of the costumes are ready, a good way of beginning the Technical is to have a costume parade. This will allow the Director,

Amplification

It may be necessary to mike some of the orchestra and also to give *portable mikes* to the singers. These will need to be inserted in the costumes, and a separate technician employed to *mix and balance the voices with the orchestra*.

Designer and Wardrobe Mistress to see all the costumes and check that everything is there. Youngsters get very excited when putting on their costumes for the first time; supervision, therefore, is essential so that they learn the correct way to put on and wear their clothes. Make a list of all the alterations that need to be done. If these are extensive then the actor may not be able to have his or her costume for the technical rehearsal so that someone can work on it. Once the costume parade is over the technical rehearsal can commence.

STANDING BY

Everyone is told to go to their opening positions and to 'stand by'. There should only

be one voice at the Technical – that is, the Stage Manager's – who will then explain what needs to happen. This section may encompass a few cues and a page of text. The company goes through this section and then a halt is called. The Director then discusses any changes that need to take place, and it will be rehearsed again. This will be repeated until all the problems are ironed out. And in like manner we move on through the play.

DRESSERS

If there are tricky costume changes they need to be timed and help engaged if there are difficulties. The Wardrobe Mistress will have anticipated any difficulties and help will be

A half-finished costume waiting for an actor.

The final touches to a costume.

found. Actors not fully employed can be used as dressers, but once employed they must always be there to help their fellows change. Through familiarity and practice things do become quicker and more efficient, so be patient.

PLANNING AHEAD

You may have gathered that the Technical can be a long and tiring process, but it is important for the technical team to get to know the play. The actors have been rehearsing it for weeks and should be well acquainted with it, but the technicians have been working on all the other aspects of the production, and are possibly seeing the play for the first time.

The DSM can keep things together from the prompt corner by giving clear and precise calls to all the crew and cast when they are needed to stand by before their cue comes. Before you start the Technical have a good look through the text to find out everyone's availability. If there are scenes in the play with only a few characters, it may be sensible to let the bulk of the company go home rather then keep them hanging about waiting. If there is time, take two days over the Technical so that people are fresh for the performances.

If you choose to keep all the company on stage during the whole performance, let the technical side be as simple as possible, and let them become responsible for the changes in focus. Make sure when plotting the lights that the scenes that will happen in front of the company will need to be lit from the side, top and back. This will have the effect of putting anyone upstage in shadow. Have a home base for those people not employed in the action. Actors off-stage often want to watch the action from the side, but they can become a distraction and also get in the way of scene changes. Once the play is in performance, the main consideration has to be the audience's pleasure and enjoyment.

A good thorough technical rehearsal is worth three poor dress rehearsals and will pay dividends in the long run.

AT THE END OF THE DAY

Gather everyone together to thank them for the day's work. Make sure that they have hung up their costumes and put the smaller items into their shoe bags. Remind them to find and put their scripts in a safe place. Give them clear instructions about when they are needed again and what they should bring with them. If it is late, make sure that everyone has transport to get home. Try to be punctual as parents and guardians will be waiting to collect their sons and daughters. Let everyone find a still, silent moment to let the excitement and events of the day pass before they leave the space.

The technical team might have some work to do, but after a long day everyone will need some rest. The wardrobe department could have some washing to do, and that needs to be collected and sorted. Check with your Stage Manager about when to call the actors as they will need to have a physical and vocal warm-up before the dress rehearsal and the stage may be needed for technical work. The night after the Technical is often used by the designer to paint the stage and rostra, so that it will be dry before the next day's rehearsal.

THE FIRST DRESS REHEARSAL

Dress rehearsal day has to be calm and disciplined as everyone will be nervous and excited, some young actors may be quite tearful and everyone will be tired from the night before. A good way to start is to have a brief company conversation about how they felt the technical rehearsal had gone. These meetings will often happen in the auditorium. Ask them to sit as a company and not sprawl

133

about. They need to be constantly reminded that they should respect the theatre and the performing space.

This meeting will give rise to observations about focus and noise and lack of discipline, and as it will come from them, you will be able to make your own observations as to how you perceived the day had gone. Don't let them get away with shoddy behaviour, or excessive showing off. Remind them about the importance of listening to everything and of speaking clearly, for and to everyone in the space. With the excitement of costumes and lighting and the all-important audience just around the corner, they will need to give themselves a personal direction for the day.

Your Assistant Director or an older and responsible member of the company may need to take the warm-up. Once their voices and bodies are ready they should go quietly to prepare for the dress rehearsal. You might want to look at some moments in the play to make an adjustment or to see a crucial scene in the play. Let them go to their dressing rooms and wait for the DSM to call them to the stage.

The dress rehearsal can be stopped at any time, but only if something crucial has gone wrong or if actors may be in danger of injuring themselves. By this time in the proceedings you should have weaned yourself from herding the company like a sheepdog, and have allocated that responsibility to someone

Meg Jepson giving notes after a dress rehearsal.

else, for as Director you need to be in the audience watching the performance to see that all is going well. Have a pad and pencil with you at all times and make notes. You might think that you will remember all the things that go wrong but you won't. You are not only watching the actors' performances but also what is happening with the lights and sound, with the scene changes and the look of the costumes, at a chair that has been put in the wrong place, or someone standing in the wings waiting to enter.

RECORDING DETAILS OF THE 'DRESS'

Make sure that the DSM times the play, all the acts and the interval, and makes out a report sheet that should be completed for every dress rehearsal and all the performances. It should show the timing of the acts and interval; the things that have gone wrong like missed sound cues; late entrances; excessive noise in the wings; forgotten props and people coming on to the stage from the wrong entrance.

After the dress rehearsal the cast should go and change into their everyday clothes, hang up their costumes and return any props they have used to the prop table. Giving out extensive notes after a dress rehearsal is not a

Accident Book

It is important to keep an accident book for your own and the company's well-being. If something happens to one of the members – for instance, a fall resulting in a twisted ankle – it could be wrongly diagnosed and develop into something more serious. If the accident goes unrecorded and the injured party sues your company, you could become liable for costly compensation.

good idea. The actors need reassurance and a clear direction to go home with. You will need to give your notes to the technical team before they go home, they may even have to work on the set and lights. Some lighting designers like to adjust their lighting during the first dress rehearsal so they may have to do some refocusing or rehanging of lamps once the stage is cleared.

PHOTO CALL

In order to have a record of your production it is a good idea to have some photographs taken. The theatre you are performing in might have front-of-house display boards specially designed for this purpose. There are different ways in which photos can be taken. The first is a set of photographs depicting dramatic moments from the play. Your photographer may want you to put the actors into suitable poses that he will then photograph. This can lead to rather wooden pictures, and fail to capture the atmosphere of the production. However, if you do decide to go with this idea, make a list of scenes you want taken and arrange the photo call to happen before one of your dress rehearsals. Arrange the poses you want photographed to be shot in reverse order so that the cast will end up dressed in their first-act costumes, ready for the run-through.

The other alternative is for your photographer to take pictures during the dress rehearsal. Some people are very good at doing this and manage to enter the action without disturbing the actors. The cast often respond well to this method, and it gives them a very strong focus of concentration. You will end up with some excellent shots. There may be trouble with the darker lit scenes. However, an experienced photographer will bring along more than one camera with different films and lenses.

Photo call.

THE SECOND DRESS REHEARSAL

You may not always have the luxury of a second dress, and if there is one scheduled it will often take place on the afternoon of the first performance which is not a good idea. If you have a choice, and the first dress has gone quite smoothly it is better to work some scenes rather than go for a full dress. In the previous chapter I suggested that all the notes were written out on large pieces of paper and fixed to the floor so that when the company arrives for notes they can read and digest them at their own speed. If notebooks have been kept during rehearsal, they should bring them along together with a pencil or pen.

Try not to let the notes session go on for too long but the company may need to be grounded, and refocused into the play, so some philosophical chat would be in keeping, reminding them of the journey the company has been on during rehearsals and where they are now in bringing their production to life. They need clear precise direction.

Time the call for notes in such a way that whatever your plans are for the day, the actors are not kept hanging about. If you go with the second dress they will need a good warm-up. The company will be tired and nervous so breathing, stretching and focusing should be important elements. You, the Director, should take this session, as your concentration will have been elsewhere during the last two days, so it will give you a chance to re-establish your role as Director.

By this time the production needs an

audience to listen to the play, and if you are presenting your play in your school this second dress rehearsal is a good opportunity for you to invite some of the pupils to the performance. If it is in class time you will have to get the necessary permission for your audience to miss classes. Treat the performance in the same way as the first dress, with notes maybe this time directly after the performance.

You should now be ready for the all-important first night. The whole process should be smooth and easy with a natural progression into performance. The actors should be looking forward to performing and sharing their play with generosity and love.

10 THE FIRST NIGHT AND THE RUN OF THE PLAY

Your journey to the first night could have been smooth and productive, or it could have been fraught with difficulties: with illness; members leaving because they were not happy; scenery not being ready in time; tickets not selling as swiftly as hoped. Whatever the circumstances the curtain will rise, and the lights come up on your production at seven thirty in the evening as scheduled.

If you have had a dress rehearsal that afternoon, try to schedule it early, so that the company can have a break for some refreshment and can assemble well before the half hour. Have a list of everybody at the stage door, or the equivalent, where the company can sign themselves in and out. This procedure should be established for the dress rehearsals as well, but definitely for performances. You have to know if everybody is present, and it also gives everyone personal responsibility.

THE NOTE SESSION

The pre-performance session should start with notes from the last run-through. These can be given to the whole company either verbally or if you have adopted the method of writing the notes down for them, on large sheets of paper. You need to share thoughts about how they

---

Stage Fright

Nearly everybody will suffer from a certain amount of first-night nerves. These can take the form of excitement, butterflies in the stomach, an irregular heart beat, sweaty palms and so on, but can give a great deal of energy to the performance. However, stage fright is something quite different as it can render a person frozen in their tracks, and put them into a complete state of panic, so that they forget what they have to say and do. A serious state of stage fright may mean a member of your cast not appearing at all for the performance. This is unusual but can happen especially when an individual has experienced it in another company. Keep your eyes and ears open as dealing with this early on in rehearsal can divert a disaster.

---

are feeling and how they should deal with their nerves. Some of the actors may complain of feeling ill, of a sore throat, or a pulled muscle, of sickness and headaches. These are all symptoms of nerves and though you should pay attention to them it is very likely they will have disappeared when they are dancing into the small hours at the first-night party.

COMPANY WELL-BEING AND THE ROUTINE OF PERFORMANCE

Check about what food they have taken and make sure they have all got bottles of water. Check there is plenty of paper in the loos. These will be well used. Don't let the company have any time on their hands, keep them occupied right up to the performance. A useful observation to make is the journey the actor makes between entrances. The company may have begun to notice how a routine is already being established backstage: meeting people at the same point in the play on your way to enter; waiting in the same area backstage; putting your costume change out in a specific way each time. These are good habits to be encouraged. They may contradict notes you may give about performances where you will be challenging them to be alive, to be aware and in the moment, and to keep their performances fresh.

PRE-PERFORMANCE WARM-UP

After the note session they should do a warm-up both vocally and physically. Concentrate on breathing and gentle stretching. Get them to work in pairs with a massage, but do not encourage talking or wasting energy in silly games and gossip. A game of 'he' or of throwing the ball to each other using text from the play, are useful exercises to do. Choose a short scene from the play, possibly one that has not gone very well at the last dress and let them run a section of it, then end the session with a good circle holding hands and listening.

After the warm-up they should go quietly to their dressing rooms and get ready, in plenty of time to check their props and anything else for

A simple travelling warm-up – crawling like cats.

Dead legs.

Warming up the feet.

which they have responsibility. It is amazing how first-night nerves can disturb their routine. Try to leave them alone in their preparation for the performance, and let stage management look after them and their discipline.

COMMUNICATING WITH STAGE MANAGEMENT

If you have any queries or adjustments make sure that your DSM knows about the change and where it is to happen. The DSM has to cue all the effects, and if one is altered or cut he or she has to know about it. Remind your Stage Manager who is responsible for discipline backstage to keep the actors away from peering front of house to see if they can locate their parents and friends; that silence and decorum backstage is of the utmost importance and that any untoward behaviour is entered into the show report.

ADVICE TO THE DIRECTOR BEFORE AND DURING THE FIRST PERFORMANCE

Prepare yourself for the performance. Take your notebook and pencil, and see that everything is happening front of house as it should be. There will be parents to greet, and benefactors who have lent props or donated money and materials towards the success of the production and they need to be included, and thanked. For the director the first performance is, on one hand an enormous relief, on the other hand there is no catharsis. You can see all the things that are going well, but also all the things that are going wrong, and you are no longer in a position to stop the action. Also be aware of how the audience is receiving the play and whether the actors are speaking slowly and clearly enough. You will be used to hearing the dialogue and imagining

what the finished product will be like. What you are now experiencing is the result of all your labours, so let the play now speak to you as freshly as your own nerves will allow. Unless it is absolutely necessary, do not go backstage during the interval. You may have a task to do, if not leave the company in the safe hands of others, and circulate round the audience to eavesdrop on how they are experiencing the performance. Feedback from an audience is very important.

AFTER THE PERFORMANCE

Instruct the Stage Manager that after the curtain call the actors return to their dressing-rooms and get changed as soon as possible into their everyday clothes and to gather as a company either on stage or wherever appropriate. There should be no running out to speak to friends and relatives. Meet the company, thank them for their work and make suitable encouraging, or if necessary truthful observations about the performance. It is up to the Director's discretion how long or detailed this note session should be, but parents will be waiting to take their children home, the company will be tired, and so will you, and very little of what you say will sink in. Arrange a sensible time for notes on the following day before the next performance. Without being a killjoy try to avoid a first-night party, as some of your cast may have to be in school the next morning at 8.30 or 9.00, and others may have to be at work.

THE SECOND NIGHT

Many people dread the second night almost as much as the first but with a different kind of apprehension. This is quite natural because the wonder and excitement that the company have actually got through the play, and with an audience, is an achievement in itself, but to

The Tempest, *Sheffield Youth Theatre. The court and the spirits of the island.*

*The court devour
Ariel's banquet.*

The need for live music.

repeat the whole experience, well, that seems to be almost impossible. When you come to look through your notes on the first-night performance you may not even be able to read the illegible scribble. It is often at five o'clock in the morning that you get a much clearer picture of what went on. First nights are often rushed, noisy, and with no proper listening. Adrenalin makes the actors trigger-happy. The opposite can happen when the nerves affect the breathing so that lines fade towards the end, and a slowing down in pace almost brings the play to a halt. Even if the performance went well in terms of pace and clarity it is as well to remind the company of these things during the note session.

THE NOTE SESSION

Give yourself a good hour and a half before the second performance for the note session. With encouragement and careful preparation the second performance can often be very good – cooler and less exciting, perhaps, but often clearer and better paced. The company will be tired, for performing is an exhausting experience both mentally and physically. Some people might be thinking, 'that's it,' and have no enthusiasm to do it again.

There are also the comments from those who saw the first night, from the adoring mother who thinks her son was easily the best, to the best friend who could have been in the play but decided against it, and is full of criticism. Some of the comments may be very valid, and should be considered, but the last thing the company needs is to have its morale upset. It's good to hear some of these comments at the note session because a drastically altered performance that suddenly appears on the second night without any warning can disturb the whole company, and is often the result of some badly informed friend/critic giving their opinion. Your skill and tact in giving accurate feedback will be heard and acted on by a well-prepared company of young actors.

THE WARM-UP

A vigorous and full warm-up is often a good idea. Some of the older members will have had their own celebrations regardless of any warning you might have delivered the night before. They will need plenty of water and some exercise to get their circulation going, and to rid their systems of any toxins that may be lurking there.

If any scenes have been particularly slow, try to pinpoint the moment when this started to happen, and choose a good moment just before this and just run that section. It's good to rehearse small sections at the warm-up. Do a good vocal warm-up with lots of massaging of the face and humming. If there are songs they should be sung and harmonies checked. Be detailed in everything you do.

THE WORD RUN

It can happen that there is a gap between the first and second performances. This can be in your favour but it is sometimes necessary to have a word run. These are quite difficult to manage because some people are kept waiting around before it comes to their scenes. It is a chance for everyone to hear the play again in a concentrated form. It is also an opportunity to check on accuracy concerning the text. The DSM will often be given the responsibility of taking this rehearsal and it can develop into a slack and useless exercise, which is not only bad for morale and discipline but also undermines the hard work already invested in the production, and is bad manners to those who have heavy responsibilities. You may have doubly cast the play in some of the larger roles and the second night could be their turn to perform.

Get everyone sitting either in chairs or on the floor, but not lolling about or lying around the floor or on each other. Do not allow eating or smoking and get the actors to address the text to the person to whom they are speaking. Have a member of the company or stage management watch the text and make notes where inaccuracies are taking place. After the word run the actors need to find out where they are making mistakes. It is sometimes necessary to stop the word run to sort out a piece of text that has gone awry.

THE PRESS AND MEDIA

It is possible either through your invitation or because of interest in your production that your local paper will want a press photo. This could accompany an article about the company or even a criticism that would appear later in the week. There may be a local actor in whom they are interested or one of your actors who is about to appear on television. Make arrangements for the press to take their photos either before a dress rehearsal or the first night. Do not allow this to interfere with your schedule, just make room for it. The session will be very like the one I described in Chapter 8 and should not last more than twenty minutes. Make sure that those people needed are informed in advance. The Wardrobe Department will also need to know as will Stage Management.

In the event of a press interview either with you or any member of the company, it is as well to remember that though most publicity is good and positive, be very careful about what you say. A badly worded quote out of context may make a good headline for the reporter but may not do your production any favours. Also make sure that these interviews do not affect your schedule, as at this stage of the production time is extremely precious.

Make sure that you speak to the company about broadcast and written criticism of the production. Good and bad notices may draw the public's attention to the production but may in no way reflect its quality. It is only one person's opinion after all. We are all very sensitive to adverse criticism especially when it appears in print.

THE REST OF THE RUN

You will need to prepare your company for every performance in order to keep the play in good order. Your actors will have had no training, just the preparation period that you have had with them. Some will have worked with other youth theatre companies that have approached rehearsal and performance in a different way. Every night one or more

Paulina and Antigonus in **The Winter's Tale.**

members of the company will have friends and relatives in to watch, some people may come twice to see the play, so it has to be kept up to scratch.

THE LAST PERFORMANCE

Some people like to play tricks on the final performance of a play or musical; this should be discouraged at all costs. The last performance should receive as much care in its preparation as the first. The attention to detail in working with your group requires a great deal of personal discipline, but your integrity and example will reflect in the attitude and application of the company. If members find it too hard for them, or no longer fun, then maybe they have chosen the wrong group. On the other hand, be sure that you are not becoming set and humourless in your ambition to run the perfect company.

Bohemia in **The Winter's Tale.**

The Dream alfresco.

Sadly, the last performance of the play is often not the best that the company will give. It may lack balance and flow, either through tiredness or trying too hard and the pace becomes slow and heavy. There is a need for some company members to make a quick getaway, but make sure that you all meet as a company after the curtain call to say goodbye to the play, to thank them all for their work, and to make sure that you have some volunteers to help with the get out.

Time to Clear up

Costumes have to be collected, washed or cleaned and stored for future use. Props that have been borrowed or hired have to be

returned. The set has to be disposed of or stored. The scripts have to be collected if hired (especially musical scores) and sent back to the owners. The theatre or hall has to be left as it was found. In some cases this will have to happen after the last performance or it could be delayed until the next day. The technicians will have to dismantle their lights and return those borrowed or hired. Steel decking rostra that has been hired will need to be collected and returned. You may find that your garage becomes the refuge for props and sets that you wish to keep for future use.

Post-Production Meeting

Let us hope that your production proves to be successful. Some of the young actors will have experienced their first taste of being part of a youth theatre production, and will want the play to go on for longer, but all good things have to come to an end and life has to return to the normal routine. But you should be looking ahead. All those people involved in helping to realize the production may also feel that there is something lacking in their lives and there are practical matters to attend to.

The Financial Position

The treasurer will have to work out how the production has done financially, whether it has come within, below or over budget, and whether the box office receipts are above or below the estimate you made when planning the production all those months ago. A meeting of everybody concerned plus representation from the cast is needed to gain a practical feed-back session.

Raising More Money

If the company is in deficit, a decision has to be made as to how to deal with this, and your fund-raisers may have to organize some event to reduce this. However, the Youth Theatre may have acquired some assets in the form of costumes and scenery that were either made for the production or given by a generous benefactor.

RETURNING BORROWED ITEMS

Make sure that all the borrowed items have been returned in good order. Goodwill and respect from the local community are essential, and remember you are supplying a much-needed local amenity for the well-being of the young people of your area.

COSTUME CARE

Costumes that have been specially made for the production are cleaned and stored somewhere accessible.

THE NEXT EVENT

It is not necessary to start planning another full-scale production. You will need time to reflect on what has happened, but you will also be aware of hidden talents within the company, actors who have suddenly blossomed during the performances in what seemed small parts. Also your leading performers may now be on the way to university, or are worried about the workload at school as important exams loom. However, there can be a regular series of classes and workshops that can be planned for one night a week or every fortnight. The friendships that have been forged often continue into later life; on the other hand, some people go out in adulthood with renewed

confidence, but may never want to act again.

The meetings of the Youth Theatre must not be just a social event. The nature of the workshops and session should enhance the work and discoveries made during your rehearsal process. New members might want to be part of the organization after seeing your production, and they need to be introduced to your working methods. Those older members might want to develop their own teaching skills so that they can work with younger members who want to join the Youth Theatre. A small nominal payment may be necessary to help with the expense of keeping the organization running, and you may have a demanding job that will take up your time and energy.

Keep your ears and eyes open for yourself for courses and workshops you may attend that you see advertised locally or hear about taking place in London, or in your nearby city. There are always new things to learn, voice exercises, developing devising skills, and the many movement techniques now being taught. It is always good to get amongst people who are doing the same work as you are, to hear how they cope with their successes and failures and to share ideas about choices of material.

You could use your local church for a Christmas event with carols, and the story of the nativity, giving the company an opportunity to develop their devising skills without having the pressure of a full-scale production. Whatever the outcome of your production do not underestimate the pleasure, comradeship and confidence your production has given to everyone concerned.

Show Report
Marat Sade

Number: Dress 1
Date: 03/07/02
DSM: Ian White
Crew: Laura Cox SM, Harry Guthrie ASM, Karen Philips ASM, Ollie Jeffrey LX, OP,
Woody Woodcock Production LX

House percentage: N/A

	Up	Down	Time
Act I	19.50	21.01	1hr 11min
Interval	21.01	21.17	16min
Act II	21.17	21.53	36min
Total running time:			2hr 3min
Total playing time:			1hr 47min

Technical observations

Columier's light came on before LX cue 4. His seat is empty before this point. The level was also inconsistent.

The cloth slide became detached, Mr Ash held this in place.

LX cue 21 seemed out of place. Please will you confirm this, Adrian.

DSM mistakenly gave two 'go's on LX cue 45. LX Op returned to cue 45 and continued running as normal.

House lights came up on LX cue 9.

The schoolmistress's glasses were not set. These have been added to the setting list.

Performance Observations

Miss Smith's line 'Four years after the Bastille fell' became 'Four years after remember how'. As a consequence the song did not scan properly.

The guards replaced the black cloth on the guillotine back to front.

Mr Bennett's opening line in Marat's Liturgy 'Remember how it used to be' became 'Remember how it was'.

Distribution: Laura Cox, Harry Guthrie, Karen Philips, Woody Woodcock, Ollie Jeffrey, Toby Sedgwick, Adrian Hall, Matt Harris, Jacqui George, Caroline Heale, Paul McConkey

A show report.

Stageworks Autum 2002
(Sheffield Youth Theatre's Acting Class and Theatre Workshop)
22/09/02

Dear

Thank you for booking a place with Stageworks. The first session starts on Saturday 28 September and takes place at the Victoria Hall, Norfolk Street, Sheffield City Centre, opposite the Crucible Theatre. Please enter by the side entrance on Chapel Walk; follow the signs to the top of the building where you will find the Youth Theatre's studio. Sessions start at 10.00am and end at 12 noon. Please arrive a little early on the 28th to allow for registration and payment of fees. The balance of fee (£40 or the prearranged concessionary payment) is payable at this time, in full; cash or cheques can be accepted and cheques should be made payable to 'String of Pearls'.

Clothing should be loose-fitting and allow maximum movement (please see enclosed picture for guidance). Large pieces of jewellery, such as long earrings, bracelets or necklaces should be removed for the sessions, for the welfare of the participant. Mobile phones are not allowed in the studio during work time but can be left in the adjacent Green Room, which is locked. We also advise you against bringing anything of value to these sessions.

The sessions follow consecutively up to and including 16 November when the students will give an informal presentation of the term's work. Students pursuing Stageworks find the work to be very beneficial – the raising of confidence is only one area that can be improved. The Youth Theatre specializes in voice work and provides each student with individual attention to develop and strengthen his or her voice. The Art of Acting requires a number of skills that hang on the level of concentration of the individual. Students who work with us for a period of time report increased academic capacity and ease as a result of the time we spend in developing this ability.

We have to underline that all these things *take time* to achieve, which is why we do *not return the fee*. Students cannot know the full benefit of what they have received until the final session has taken place and the informal presentation provides the necessary challenge to reveal what has developed. Participants are often pleasantly surprised! If you have any further questions please don't hesitate to contact me at this telephone number: 0114 2882929.

All good wishes,

(Meg Jepson, Artistic Director, SYT)

Stageworks.

GLOSSARY OF THEATRICAL TERMS

Apron is that area of the stage that protrudes into the audience beyond the setting line.

Auditorium is the place where the audience sits.

Bars are the metal poles that comprise part of the flying system to which the scenery is attached.

Blacks refer to the black drapes that are hung around the stage to give a black neutral setting.

Book is another name for the prompt copy.

Brace is the support attached to the scenery to help it stand up.

Borders are strips of material or long thin flats covered in material that are hung above the stage to hide the backstage machinery in the grid, technical equipment, and all the lights suspended on bars.

Calls refer to the verbal and written instructions given by the stage management to the cast, crew and audience about the commencement of performances and also

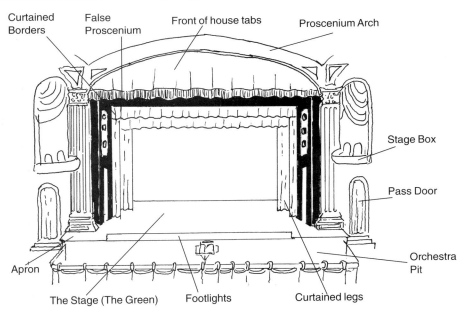

Conventional stage as seen by the audience.

about rehearsal times.

Counterweights are specially shaped weights that are used to balance the weight of scenery that is flown up into the space above the stage.

Cyclorama can either be made of plaster and be a permanent fixture or is a curved cloth of white canvas that is hung and stretched across the back of the stage.

Dock is the place where the scenery is kept. The name is a hangover from the days when sailors were used to help with the backstage scene shifting.

Dock Doors are the doors from the stage to the outside that are used when scenery built outside the theatre has to be brought onto the stage, and through which a touring company

The dock doors at the Yvonne Arnaud Theatre, Guildford.

will unload their set.

Drapes are the name given to sets of black or grey curtains used to create a neutral setting.

Dressing refers to objects that adorn the set but are not part of the action, for example curtains at the window, coatpegs on the back of the door, pictures on the wall, to give the set a lived-in look.

Dry will happen when an actor forgets his lines and is unable to continue.

Flats are the flat pieces of scenery made of wood and canvas and then painted to look like wallpaper, a forest or whatever the designer wants them to look like.

Fly Tower is the space above the stage where scenery can be hung, stored and flown. In the early theatre these were operated by ropes and pulleys, and needed several men to lift one large cloth. But nowadays they are composed of metal poles, wires, and a complex system of pulleys and counterweights that can be operated by one man or a motor.

Footlights are hardly used today and are a strip of lights at stage level set in the very front of the stage to light the faces from below.

Gels are the name given to the coloured gelatine filters that are used to put colour into the lights.

Gods is the name given to the highest tier in

*The tramp's hut, **The Sea** by Edward Bond, set by Barry Jarvis. Photo: Mark Dean*

the auditorium, and is usually where the cheapest seats in the house are.

Green Room is a retiring room for the actors originally right next door to the stage, which was called the **Green** (a place where people play, and the central focus of a village community).

Grid refers to the grid of metal or wood rafters in the roof of the stage which supports the flying system.

Ground Plan is a scaled plan of the stage onto which the designer will draw where his set will be. The positions of the fly bars are also shown on the plan as is the wing space, dock doors and exits to the other parts of the theatre.

Ground Row is the name given to a strip of scenery to mask lights that are being used to illuminate the bottom of the cyclorama.

The **Half** is the first call to be made before a performance and is timed at 35 minutes before curtain up. Three more calls are made after this, the **Quarter,** the **Five** and **Beginners** which is five minutes before curtain up. In the theatre there is a formality about these calls in which the actors are referred to as Mr and Miss, the Ladies and Gentlemen of the Orchestra and so on.

Iron is the fireproof metal curtain that is lowered in the event of a fire breaking out backstage to protect the audience. By law it should be lowered and raised once every performance in full view of the audience.

Lamps are the lights that are used to illuminate the stage.

Lantern is situated in the roof of the stage like a small greenhouse, which, in the event of a fire, opens up like a flue to draw the flames away from the auditorium.

Legs are the curtained wings that are hung down either side of the stage in order to mask off the wing space.

Limes are the powerful front-of-house hand-operated spotlights that are used in musicals,

opera and ballet to pick out the leading characters.

Masking refers to flats or drapes that hide the backstage area from the audience's view.

Pass Door is the door connecting the stage with the auditorium. This door is only used by stage management, authorized front-of-house staff, and actors who need to make entrances from the auditorium.

Prompter is the person who follows the play in the **Prompt** script and sits in the **Prompt Corner** (the other side of the stage is called the **OP**, opposite prompt); if an actor dries then he will feed him the next line. This is one of the tasks that the DSM has to fulfil.

Lamps.

The lantern at the Yvonne Arnaud Theatre.

Props is the shortened version of the word 'properties' and refers to the objects needed other than scenery and costumes – for example, umbrellas, teacups and saucers, cigarette cases and so on, and can be divided into personal and hand props.

Pros is the shortened version for the proscenium arch that separates the stage from the auditorium. In the older theatres this was always decorated with gilt, plaster and statuettes.

Rake refers to an angled stage floor. Most early proscenium theatres were built with a raked floor in order to give those people sitting in the stalls a better view of the actor.

Rostrum is a permanent or collapsible raised platform that fulfils many functions. Rostra break up the flatness of the stage to give a variety of levels, and can be very useful if you have a large cast, or a play that dictates many locations that are used simultaneously. They are made in wooden sections so that they can be folded and stored. The tops are made separately and can also be used on steel decking.

Steel Decking is another base for rostra made of steel and can be hired or purchased if money permits.

Strike means to remove a chair, a prop or the whole set from the stage.

Tabs are the curtains that are flown or drawn to hide some, or all of the scenery from the audience.

153

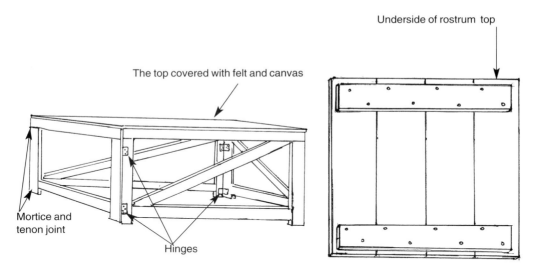

The top covered with felt and canvas

Underside of rostrum top

Mortice and
tenon joint

Hinges

A folding rostrum and top.

Ornate treads at GSA.

Tormentors are two permanent flaps just inside the proscenium arch that can help to mask the set.

Treads are the backstage steps that may be needed to get down from or up on to rostra. They can vary from a small staircase to just two steps.

Wings refers to the space on either side of the stage that are used for the storing of scenery and for a place for the performers to wait before they make their entrances. It is not essential for you to be fully acquainted with all these terms, but it will help to understand what is being communicated, especially when it comes to meetings.

INDEX